Me and My P

An itinerant architect's journal
of the 20th century

"The world is a book; he who does not travel reads only a page"
St. Augustine

Cyril Bowman

For Dympna

Who shared most of the experiences
and has lived with every paragraph

Published in Ireland by Author, The Glade, Athenry, Galway
Copyright Cyril Bowman 2004 revised edition 2015

ISBN 0-594757-10-6

Acknowlegements:

This book is a personal journal of my experiences, while working and travelling throughout Africa and Asia

The photographs are my own except the following:

Mopti Mosque – MacDonald's Encyclopaedia of Africa
Earthen architecture on the Niger –Air France
Brasilia Cathedral – Brazil Tourist Web-site
Sydney Opera House – Pictorial Souvenir Book
Tilla-Kari interior – Uzbektourism
Landmines – CMAC Cambodia

I would like to thank the following, for reading the early drafts, their honest and invaluable comments, guidance and suggestions as friends:

George N Allen, WashingtonDC
Richard Heaver, Goa, India
Tom May, Cong, Mayo
Derry O'Connor, Galway
Isabel Ortiz, Manila
Stan Scheyer, Virginia, USA

Of course, I especially thank my wife Dympna who inspired and encouraged the work throughout.

I have worked with some wonderful people and I would like to mention those sadly deceased early of whom I have fond memories:

Lamine Diouf, Paris
Lina Domingo, WashingtonDC
Althea Hill, Washington, DC

Ar dheis De go raibh a hanam dhilis"

The author was born in London and raised in Ireland. He was educated by the Christian Brothers and at the National University of Ireland where he graduated in Architecture and Law.

He worked in West Africa for some years and on his return, commenced practice as an architect in Galway.
He was also a consultant to the International Development Banks for many years on projects in Africa and Asia.

He is now retired and lives in Ireland and France.

By the same author:

'A Palatine Story'
&
"Christianity: The East/West Divide"

Contents:

AUTHOR'S NOTE

Towards the end of the twentieth century, as I retired from architectural practice and hung up my pencil, the first of my grandchildren arrived to dwell in the new millennium.

The co-incidence led me to reflect on the vast changes, in all areas of life, that occurred during my century and to wonder what the new century might hold for them.

Born in the 1930s and having lived through most of the twentieth century, it occurred to me that in the normal course of events, my grandchildren will see most of the twenty-first century. While we cannot know what the new century will hold for them, the future in general flows from the past and this prompted me to set down for my grandchildren, the story of my century. The problem of course was how to do it !

Eventually, I decided to write this journal, not of my life as such but of one single thread which flowed through the century; my work in the Developing World.The intention is to weave my way from country to country so that each chapter should become like a distinct new canvas of that particular time.

The descriptive images here are intended to present my experiences like a collage of the twentieth century.

The historic background is given for each country together with its economic and social circumstances in order to illustrate where they were at that time and to this mix I have added some of my own personal experiences.

Cyril Bowman, Galway. Ireland

ME AND MY PENCIL 2

An Itinerant Architect's Journal of the 20th century

INTRODUCTION

My story starts at home in Ireland where the circumstances of the people, at the beginning of the twentieth century, were poor. The politics of the nineteenth century were seen to have failed and the only bright stars were the Gaelic and Literary revivals of the early century which became the major influences for the future. The subsequent War of Independence led to the establishment of the present State in 1921. Throughout the world too, at the beginning of the 20th century, the colonized status of Asia and Africa was the accepted norm and following the defeat of Germany in 1914, their colonies were simply divided like chattels without question between the victors Britain and France.

The early decades of the century saw two world wars, separated by an economic depression and these events changed the world, in the words of WB Yates following the 1916 rising in Dublin

"A terrible beauty is born".

In Ireland the 1914-1918 World War coincided with the Rising for Independence successfully achieved for 26 of the 32 counties in 1920. During the Second World War 1939-1945 Ireland, was one of the five militarily neutral countries of Europe. That period was known as *"The Emergency"* in Ireland during which time we remember ration cards, fine summers, fathers' coloured pins moving across the maps of Europe and the islands of the Pacific meticulously displayed on the walls.

The modern era in Europeconsequently began after the wars towards the middle of the century.

It is difficult to visualise the world of the 1950s. It was a time of reconstruction after the devastation of the Second World War and the victorious Generals Eisenhower and de Gaulle were elected Presidents of the US and France respectively. In Ireland, Eamon de Valera, one of the leaders of the War of Independence, was elected President.

The world had been changed radically by the destruction of war in which subject peoples discovered that their colonial masters were unable to protect them at such times. They realized that in future they must depend on their own resources. Asia experienced occupation, destruction, liberation and independence while in the words of the British Prime Minister, Harold Macmillan, the winds of change were blowing across Africa too, where leaders like Nkruma and Toure, were leading independence movements.

Communications in Ireland was *'another world'*. In 1949 there were on average twenty three telephone calls per person per year or one call every two weeks and many of these, including local calls, were manually operated by winding a handle at the side of the instrument with each requiring operator intervention. The corresponding figures in 1996 were over 2,000 calls per person per year, excluding mobile telephones or six calls per day all automatic perhaps to the far ends of the earth. There was one television for every fifteen people in 1958 receiving only British channels as the National station only commenced in 1961. By 1995 there was one TV license for every four people.

Motorcars only came into Ireland in any number after the Second World War so by 1968 there was one car per 8.6 persons and in 1998 there was one car for every 3. Air-travel too was still in it's infancy, in 1949 there were 17,000 flights in and out of Dublin carrying a quarter of a million passengers while in 1998 there were 162,000 flights carrying four million people. The flight to Londontook two and an half-hours and today it takes less than one hour.

I think I got the travel-bug in the 1940s listening to the BBC radio two-way family favourites program with their "bumper-bundle" for listeners in exotic sounding places like Trincomalee and Bangalore. I remember too cousin

George arriving in Dunmore in the late 1940s after he had gone to work in the United Nations Office in Paris. I was very impressed by his travels to the 60 Member Countries of that time. Following my 1957 graduation from University College Dublin as an architect, I worked for a few years in Belfast and Dublin during which time Dympna and I were married. I was very lucky to get a temporary job, in what was known as an un-established position, in the airport office of a Government Department because the economy in Ireland was stagnant and emigration was rampant. However, it was not long before I started to cast my eyes after opportunities overseas and soon I attended for interview at the British Colonial Office in London. They were recruiting architects for overseas contract positions for the transition period from Empire to Independence. Thus began a working relationship with both Africa and Asiathat was to span the following forty years.

At the Colonial Office they offered a choice of positions in British Guiana or Nigeria and I chose the latter because Nigeria was better known in Ireland due to the work of Irish Christian missionaries. From my inquiries too it seemed a larger and more dynamic country and seemed to offer more opportunities to a young architect. Besides, Africa did fascinate us. Most of our shops possessed a charity box inviting "donations for the black babies" and the head of the child would nod to acknowledge each penny

I still have the 1959 letters from the Colonial Office stating "I am directed by Mr. Secretary, Lennox-Boyd to ---"and the later letter of appointment from Mr. Secretary Macleod in an "On Her Majesty's Service" envelope. Dympna and I packed all our belongings, including the good china and glass crystal we hadreceived as wedding presents, into a large tin trunk and set off, with great excitement from the North Wall on the River Liffey in Dublin for Liverpool to join the Elder Dempster Line m.v Aureol on her 74th voyage on her way to Nigeria in March 1960 to the tears of some elderly relatives who feared we could be eaten in "Darkest Africa"

It was normal to travel to Africa by sea at that time and on our arrival at Liverpool docks, we went aboard the 14,000 ton passenger ship and were taken, by African stewards in immaculate white uniforms, to the first class stateroom 25 on deck D. The voyage of 6,694 km took 13-days with visits to ports of call en route including Las Palmas-Grand Canary Island, Freetown-Sierra Leone, and Takoradi-Ghana before our final arrival at Apapa, Lagos.

address your reply to
THE DIRECTOR
OF RECRUITMENT
(Overseas Service Division)
and quote the following number:

COLONIAL OFFICE

GREAT SMITH STREET, LONDON W.1
Telephone: Abbey 1266 Ext.

BCD/P 18281

22 April, 1959.

Sir,

     I am directed by Mr. Secretary Lennox-Boyd to refer to your application for an overseas appointment and to invite you to attend at this Office at 2.30 p.m. on Monday the 4th May for an interview, bringing with you samples of your recent drawings.

     A travel warrant for your journey from Holyhead to London and return is enclosed, and this should be returned if you travel by air or are unable to keep the appointment. You will be able to claim later for your second class railway fare in Ireland, for your cross channel passage at saloon rates and for an allowance of 30/- for each night necessarily spent away from your home in connection with the interview. If you travel by air to suit your own convenience you will normally be entitled to claim the equivalent of sea and rail fares and one night's subsistence allowance. It is regretted that it will not be possible to defray any other expenses incurred in attending the interview.

     You are requested to inform the Director of Recruitment as soon as possible whether you will be able to attend at the time stated, quoting the above reference number.

            I am, Sir,
            Your obedient servant,

D. A. Pollingridge (Mrs).

N. F. BOWMAN, ESQ.

Colonial Office letter, London April 1959

There were over two hundred first class and one hundred cabin class passengers on board and the program of events scheduled for the cruise included treasure hunts around the ship, housie-housie in the smoke room, scrabble in the card room, sport and deck games, competitions and race meetings. There was a carnival evening, special dinners and dances, programs for the children and Mass or Services in the library. The menus had a delightful mixture of temperate and tropical climate food and all the events were targeted to while away the thirteen days at sea as we traveled into the unknown. In addition the stateroom had toilet and shower en-suite so baths were regulated by a timesheet and the steward would knock on the cabin door when the bathroom was prepared and he had run the water.

March rarely provides ideal sea conditions and the Bay of Biscay drove most of the passengers to their cabins. During the first days, morning coffee and afternoon tea were the norm and early on the fifth day we approached Las Palmas as the island hills, with white houses and red roofs rising above a sea mist were bathed in sunshine. It looked like fairyland to us through our stateroom portholes.

After departing Las Palmas, the deck covers were removed from the swimming pool and ice cream was offered as an alternative to coffee and tea, as we sailed below 30 degrees latitude.

Each morning, we received a newsletter from the radio room updating us on current events. However, the morning news could be quite old by to-day's standard of instant coverage. As an example, one morning the newsletter giving the BBC news for that day, announced the Sharpville massacre by the South African police, of black resistance to the pass-laws which required non-whites to return each evening to colored locations. News of the event had taken ten days to filter to the media. On the ninth day we arrived in Freetown and had our first taste of Africa. From here the ship took on "deck passengers" who were allocated some confined deck space to the stern where they lived, eat and slept for their short passage.

We teamed up with a few other passengers and went ashore eager to see everything possible. It was strange to stand in the center of town by the large 500 year old cotton tree under which Africans had been sold into slavery for passage to the Americas and with which we were very familiar from the early Sierra Leone postage stamps,.

In Freetown too we called to greet the Archbishop, who years earlier as a student had been the Deacon at a funeral Mass for my uncle Joseph, a member of the Holy Ghost Order. Dr Thomas J. Brosnahan took us around the hills of Freetown to show us the houses of the wealthy owners and managers of the diamond mines - what a contrast to the corrugated iron and cardboard shacks of the majority living beside open drains in the town.

The m v Aureol in 1960   *The Cotton Tree Freetown Sierra Leone*
where Africans had been sold into slavery

One of our companions that day was a very affable priest, Father Hugh Garman, who was bound for the Augustinian monastery in Yola, Northeast Nigeria. It is sad to think that only nine years later he was slain on the altar there while saying Sunday morning Mass by a deranged man and for no apparent reason.

Outside Freetown we visited Lumley beach, probably the finest in West Africa, where some years later we were to spend an afternoon playing with our eldest son Gerard. Freetown, as an introduction to Africa was always a great shock to the newcomers and on returning to the ship we discovered that none of the long-term expatriates, known as "old-coasters", would go ashore. Instead they loved to stand by the deck-rail and watch the reaction of the newcomers as they returned to the ship. Many of us began to wonder at that stage what was ahead of us since here was a capital city on the coast and we were to go to a provincial city 1000 km upcountry.

Most of the passengers were government employees and about the tenth day of the voyage, government postings were displayed outside the bursar's office. I was to go to the architects' office in the Ministry of Works, Kaduna as was another passenger, so I set off to find him. It turned out that Harry Barnes had been through the Second World War in South-east Asia in the 1940s and was now changing from an earlier appointment in the Solomon Islands. He was being posted to the education section and I to the health program of the Ministry of Works. The next port of call Takoradi was a busy well equipped, orderly and impressive port of working derricks in the newly independent Ghana. This eased our anxiety and on the 13th day we arrived at Apapa, Lagos, Nigeria full of excitement and expectation. My tour of duty in Africa had begun.

It is interesting to reflect that North America, 5,000 km across the Atlantic and discovered by Europeans only four centuries earlier, had evolved into one of the most developed parts of the world while Africa, our closest neighbor with only 12 km of sea between us, remained the "Dark Continent". As the process of development evolved in the Americas, life in the interior of Africa remained largely unchanged and the essential character of it's vast tropical landscape unknown until the latter half of the nineteenth century. One explanation was that Africa had not lent itself easily to exploration. Two thousand five hundred kilometers of relentless desert stretched south from the Mediterranean Sea and the many rivers including the Nile, Niger and Congo with abundant rapids and falls, finally flowed through large stretches of flat country in deltas, forming sand-bank barriers to shipping. Great myths grew-up of a mysterious land with tales of exotic wild animals, primitive black pigmies, masked dancers and deadly endemic diseases.

Of course a major factor which contributed to the development of the Americas while at the same time devastated Sub-Sahara Africa was the notorious Slave Trade. The social system of Africa had previously been based on the economics of subsistence so that there was no wage-labor as such of a regular kind. Work practices were set by age groups or otherwise by tradition. People could arrive at a servile condition through conquest or punishment for crime. This slave or unpaid labor increased after the 15th century with the growth of trade. The resultant slave trade was carried on in many directions. Slavery could be trans-Indian Ocean to Asia, which was relatively minor in numbers or trans-Sahara to North Africa and Arabia, which was considerable. In both of these situations, the need was for housework and the slave, although unpaid lived with the household and had a status, however menial. They were used in a similar way for military service and this also gave them a status in the community.

However, with the discovery and opening-up of the Americas, slavery assumed an economic importance as the appetite for slave labor for the mines and plantations became insatiable. By the 17th century, hit and run raids along the African coast from Senegal to Angola gave way to a regular partnership in trade between European shipping and the coastal peoples. The latter acquired the necessary human "raw material" inland and held them in special secure camps along the coast pending ship arrivals. Ship surgeons examined the "merchandise" and those deemed fit were marked with the red-hot iron imprint of the purchasing company on their chest. Tens of millions of Sub-Saharan Africans were transported in inhuman conditions to the Americas while millions of others died in the process.By the 19th century, for example, half the population of Brazil alone was of African origin. The slave trade over three centuries created great wealth for Europeans, contributed greatly to the development of the Americas but devastated Sub-Saharan Africa. The sustained depopulation of Africa over that long period deprived the Continent of its' youngest and strongest men and women so that the early forms of commerce failed to emerge.

A combination of circumstances in the 19th century finally brought this appalling triangular trade - of cheap goods to Africa, slaves to the Americas and sugar, tobacco and wealth to European powers - to an end. The realization of the horrors inflicted finally emerged through the media while at the same time the industrial revolution changed the labor market needs as home skills were required for the new manufacturing industries that were emerging. The consequences of the slave trade, I believe, will remain for generations yet to come.

While North Africa had been incorporated into the Roman Empire over two thousand years ago, it was not until the 15th century that explorers from Portugal first traveled the coast of Africa, south of the Sahara. They did not penetrate the interior and it was only in the 19th century that Sub-Saharan Africa was eventually colonized by Europeans, primarily for trading in raw materials and thus it remained until well into the 20th century.

Like all young boys of the time with dreams of adventure and travel, Africa loomed large as we were familiar with the exotic wild animals in our zoos, tales of the French Foreign Legion in the desert and explorers of the interior which we learned about in school. My arrival in Africa was then, the fulfillment of those dreams. Although West Africa did not have the variety of exotic animals for which I had to wait a few years until we got to East Africa, it did not disappoint but more than made up for that in the cultural richness and variety of the peoples and festivals.

With over 100 tribes and languages, Nigeria probably owes its name to the 16th century Arab writer Leo Africanus, one of the first Moslem explorers who traveled the semi-desert Sahel savannah area just south of the Sahara and gave the River Niger its name. It was previously known as the "Nile-of -the-Soudan". Leo's visited several kingdoms of the area and described the big villages as inhabited by civilized people and foreign merchants, probably Arab or Berber. They had a developed decorative style of architecture and he said that agriculture, cattle and the slave trade flourished.

NIGERIA

Nigeria is a large country about 1,200 km square with the coastline intersected by an intricate network of creeks and rivers through a belt of mangrove forest swamp up to 100 km in depth. To the North there is a zone of tropical forest in undulating country with scattered hills which further inland, becomes more open and park-like. Further inland again it rises to an undulating plateau with hills of granite and sandstone, stretching on towards the Sahara Desert.

Nigeria has 3-distinct major cultures roughly coinciding with the Niger-Benue Rivers, which divide the country into 3-areas with a big Y which is incorporated in the National Flag. The industrious, individualistic and largely Christian Ibos in the East live in communities without administrative chiefs as such. The proud, sophisticated and most developed Yorubas, both Christian and Moslem, live in the West. Their chiefs are held in high esteem and are ornately dressed. A father's property is inherited by his sons while that of the mother goes to the daughters. The tall, slim and graceful Hausa-Fulani of the North are the Moslem ruling classes in a feudal society while the cow-Fulani are still nomadic cattle raisers who travel north and south with the rains, in search of grazing.

Mural decorations by BPO Onobrakpeya from 'Nigeria magazine' 1961

Nigeria is rich in a great variety of art forms: Nupe pottery, Benin bronzes, Ife terra cotta, Abeokuta printed cloths and weaving from Kano, cowrie shells, richly colored ceramics and brass from Bida as well as literature and architecture. Nigeria hosted the very successful Second World Black and African Festival of Arts and Culture in 1977, adopting the early 16th century ivory pendant mask worn by the Oba of Benin as it's symbol. That mask is recognized as one of the most beautiful examples of early Nigerian art.

The current area of Nigeria became an independent State in 1960. Politically, it had gone through many transformations from the first colonial administration of the Royal Niger Company, superseded in 1900 AD by the Protectorate of Northern Nigeria while the Protectorate of Southern Nigeria took the place of the Niger Coast Protectorate and Lagos became part of the South in 1906.

In 1914 Lord Lugard became the first Governor - General of Nigeria. Constitutional development progressed with regular conferences and each step increased regional autonomy towards Executive Government ending finally in Nigeria becoming an independent sovereign nation on October 1-1960 as a Federation of the 3-States of the North, East and West. The first complete census showed a 1953 population of 31.5

million and this had risen to an estimated 120 million by the year 2,000 AD making it the most populous country in Sub-Saharan Africa with about 25% of the population of the continent.

Festac symbol and modern carving in ebony
'Nigeria Magazine' cover carving by Lamidi Fakeye

On arrival in Lagos in April1960, we were taken to the Ikoyi Rest House, a well-landscaped pavilion style hotel in the Government Residential Area of the island suburb. Next day we were taken to the central train station where we were allocated a compartment for two, complete with toilet and wash basin, for the 25-hour rail journey up-country. We had two bunk beds, the upper folded-up when not required and the lower duplicated as a couch during the day. There was a central window table and a seat opposite, all amounting to very comfortable accommodation. We departed from the humid coast in the afternoon and traveled at an average speed of 40 km per hour through tropical forest catching glimpses of the native villages with children running and waving excitedly at the train. We reached the Yoruba capital before dark. Ibadan had a large railway station and we were told that it was the largest African town in Africa with a distinguished university and teaching hospital.

There was little to see when darkness fell as we dressed-up and made our way to the dining car, a colourful and romantic setting with soft table lighting, where we dined in an old-world elegance which was to disappear within the decade.

Early next morning we left the forest for more open bush country and soon we crossed the River Niger at Jebba by the large metal bridge which was shared by rail and road transport. It was the largest river we had ever seen and it looked beautiful in the colorful tropical dawn. As we traveled further north we entered the savanna land of the Hausa-speaking peoples and finally reached Kaduna Junction in the afternoon, about 600 meters above sea level.

It had been a memorable trip. The architecture of the villages had changed as we travelled further from the coast – first, 2-storey concrete dwellings with tiled or corrugated iron roofs, then single-storey rectangular concrete or mud-block units with thatched or iron roofs and finally, simple circular mud-block dwellings with thatched roofs.

Frederick Lugard, British soldier and colonist, after trying a number of sites which proved unsatisfactory one way or another, had finally selected Kaduna in 1917 to be developed as the new Capital of Northern Nigeria. Situated on a navigable tributary of the Niger, with an important Lagos to Kano rail junction, Kaduna, the plural of the word kada meaning crocodile, was an entirely artificial new town set in an area which had been devastated by the slave trade and so had no native associations. It is roughly in the center of the country, with an equitable and invigorating climate for most of the year. Lord Lugard later advocated making Kaduna the capital of the whole of Nigeria.

We were met on our arrival at Kaduna Junction by colleagues from the Ministry of Works office and taken to the expatriates' Kaduna Club for a welcoming drink. We then went on to the Government Catering Rest House where we stayed until we were allocated our own quarters. Each afternoon the Hausa traders would arrive with their selection of ebony, ivory, cow horns and wood carvings, baskets, carpets, kelims and colourful fabrics which they would spread out under the radiant flamboyant trees in front of the rest house.

Catering Rest-house Kaduna 1960

Traders outside the Rest-house

Business was often brisk although purchasing was a slow game as each side haggled until ideally both sides felt swindled at an agreed price. During their lean periods, the traders called around to the houses and apartments to stimulate business and they were always open to a little "changie-changie" by which one could barter in any commodity such as old shirts, skirts, shorts or any article one wished to get rid of for his ware.Negotiations were always enjoyable provided one approached it with good humour and plenty of time.

For the first 10 days or so, Norman and Joan Mills from Wales looked after us, transported us to the office, shop and play until we became independently mobile. Our relationship developed and our friendship has endured. The next people to arrive a year later to the MOW architects' division were the Dunsires from Scotland and we were delegated to look after them. Again, after an initial shock at being thrown together, an Irish Catholic and a Scot who had come from a strict Protestant background, we became good friends and forty years later we still communicate with Andrew and Joy regularly.

At home too Jansenism had had a considerable influence on our outlook so to move to a society that was not so inhibited was quite a change. Beside me at church on our first Sunday in Kaduna, a lady carried a child, cradled in the folds of her iborum as was normal. The priest's homily was taking a long time and the child became restless so the mother pulled the child around to feed from her breasts. Perfectly normal but quite a shock for one just arrived from the Ireland of the 1950s. During our first week, I was taken around to sign the visitors' books at the gate lodges of the Governor, Ministers of Departments and Lugard Hall, where the State receptions were held. We thus conformed to the protocol for inclusion on invitation lists for government receptions. Within two weeks we bought our first motorcar from Mandilas & Karaberis in Zaria, a new green Volkswagen beetle and celebrating the event that evening in the club, one man commented that he had fought the "Baskets" for five years and would not buy a German car. I was tempted to give him an Irish history lesson but refrained.

We were soon allocated a top floor apartment in Gwari Crescent, a four storey block with garages on the ground floor so life looked good as we settled in and started to make new friends.

Our VW in the shade of a mango tree   *Gwari Crescent, Kaduna*

With all the excitement, it was only at that stage that we became conscious of the real Africa, the sights, sounds and experiences.

The first thing we noticed was that day and night were pretty equal and that darkness comes very quickly, which was a new experience because at home we were used to having a long bright evening after a fine sunny day. Darkness falls shortly after 6.00pm with virtually no twilight and in Kaduna there was only a maximum of one-hour difference between winter and summer. At night we slept in two large three-quarter sized beds, pushed together to give plenty of space and were enclosed under a large mosquito net.

The bedroom windows were left wide open to the African night but ground floor windows had security bars for protection against wild animals or the occasional thief-man.

As one settles down at night, the sound of the last car dies away, the last radio is turned off and the last lighted window goes dark, one quickly becomes conscious of the real sounds of Africa. First one notices the chirping of crickets which seems to envelope the land. A rustle of leaves in the mango trees suggest some mysterious movement followed by strange indefinable humid smells from the vegetation. Then a strange new sound seems to come from everywhere, hesitant at first and then faster and faster - the beat of the tom-tom telling whatever story, like a song without words carried through the night and sometimes all night. The moonlit evenings were beautifully clear and bright with innumerable stars and there must be something about living close to the bush which made one wish to fill the space, which seems endless. Occasionally we would sit out on the balcony, put on gramophone records and fill the night with Suppe, Strauss or a coloratura soprano and I often wondered what the tom-tom players thought of it all.

In the film "Out of Africa", Karen Blixen said of Denys that he too even took the gramophone and Mozart records on safari. I have known engineers and administrators, who while living in the bush alone, apart from cook and steward, actually dressed formally in the evening for dinner. It was probably a question of keeping in touch with one's roots or in earlier times, of keeping sane.

There was a thriving Irish community throughout Nigeria which came together to celebrate National cultural events. Away from Ireland there was no "border" and the most enthusiastic promoters of the Saint Patrick's Day festivities were often from the North like Frank and Marlyn Ringland. Sometimes too we were joined by the Ambassador of Ireland as well as many Nigerians with Irish connections. I particularly remember the visit of Ambassador Eamonn Kennedy with his wife and his most interesting account of the intricacies involved in the formation of 'foreign Policy'

A tropical climate lends itself to an outdoor life of barbecues and garden parties. During 1960 there were many 'rummage sales' and "going away" parties for the colonial officers departing before October when Nigeria would become an Independent State.

The rummage sales were great for picking up "white-mans' toys"; gramophones, records, tennis rackets, golf and photographic equipment, all manner of house utensils, music instruments or maybe even a tropicalised piano.

For the parties it was normal to borrow coloured lighting from the Ministry of Works maintenance yard to string across the garden trees, making the occasion look very festive. Sometimes too the entrance road was lined with candles, set in paper bags one-third filled with sand to give a warm welcoming glow. Years later we tried that at home in Galway but with all the western wind it did not work very well. The stewards seemed to love the festive occasions as one might borrow additional stewards from friends when catering for larger numbers and they were particularly good for children's parties.

In the autumn of 1960 we celebrated an Irish wedding. Michael Giles had come to teach in St. John's College where Dympna taught. His fiancée Phil followed a little later. Immigration requirements were such that since she did not have a job or a return ticket, they went on her arrival to the Administration Offices for a civil wedding in order to legitimise her position as the wife of a valid resident. Next morning the wedding ceremonies were joyously celebrated at the Cathedral and the large reception was generously hosted by Vincent and Imelda Doyle at their house.

Larger social functions revolved around the Kaduna Club - tennis, social evenings and the "cads' bar" where one could frequent in shorts in the evening when more formal dress was required elsewhere. A year or two later, I joined the new golf club and settled in to a regular four-ball which lasted a couple of years. Meeting one of the group some years later we laughed when he recounted that on one occasion he set off very early one morning to drive over 300 km to be on time for the four-ball. At the southern end of Kaduna, the Army swimming pool was open to expatriates and very popular in the afternoons and on the weekends. On one occasion a snake entered the pool, causing consternation and the "troops" were called to get rid of it.

Wedding party, Kaduna 1960

Occasionally, snakes appeared on our front doorstep when the gardener would kill it with a swipe of his langa-langa. Two scorpions made their home in our garage once but generally the wildlife did not present a problem as prisoners at the jail were used to cut the grass and keep parks and road verges clean and tidy for health and environmental reasons.

There was an open-air cinema, the Radar, which featured American or British films once or twice a week but the Indian films were more popular with the Nigerians. The seated area at the back was covered while the cheap seats towards the front were open and it was an amusing experience to sit watching a movie during a tropical storm in the rainy season.

Kaduna proved to be a very pleasant provincial capital with a population of about 50,000 of which 2,000 were expatriates mostly working for government. We were to spend the following six years there very happily in the privileged lifestyle of expatriates, enjoying the local festivals. The Northern Durbar festival was a particularly colourful and exotic horse and camel charge towards the Emir by the Hausa/Fulani in a show of support.

Durbar Festival Zaria

Our life of course was artificial in many ways, children were sent home to expensive boarding schools so parents who might find it difficult to get comparable salaries at home could not leave. One colleague sent his wife home also because he thought she was becoming too enchanted with a known "Don Juan" in the club. The "old colonials" too were coming towards the end of their careers so there was great excitement among them each New Year and Queen's birthday as they awaited the Honours List. It was amusing to see the same procedure being repeated in the North of Ireland at the end of the century. Indeed, without realizing it, we were witnessing the end of that whole way of life. The Colonial Era ended, sometimes violently within the following decade as country after country achieved independence; eighteen countries of Africain 1960 alone.

One of the first items of advice we were given was that if while driving, we had an accident or hit someone in the bush, we should not stop or remain at the scene for fear of a violent emotional reaction, but proceed to the next town and report to the police there. The advice shocked us as heartless and unfriendly particularly as that town could be many miles away. Another practice we found most disconcerting was the British habit of talking in a pejorative manner about "these people" in the presence of their servants as if they were deaf or at least of no consequence. In fact some of the servants had been to mission schools and could well have been as well educated as some of their "masters" or mistresses".

Dympna once taught geography in such a school and I found it amusing to see her studying the railway system of industrial Britain in the evening so that she could teach it to a class next day. There had always been one question about Britain on the Leaving Certificate examination paper in Ireland. However, our teachers' philosophy was that to do well in that question one would need to study Britain to the same degree of detail as Ireland. They thought that a waste of time and suggested we skip that question and concentrate on the others about Ireland, Europe and the World.

We learned too not to take anything, even little things, for granted. Dympna once asked a pupil what was his Christian name and got the reply "Madam, I do not have a Christian name, I am a Moslem so Christian names became First names. The colour "orange" did not translate because oranges in Nigeria were green. Similarly "grapes" to us were understood as "grapefruit" locally. Our normal diet of food did not have the same nutritional value and needed to be augmented with vitamins and minerals. Eggs were tiny from guinea hens and powders such as flour had to be sieved to remove weevils. Each year before the rains would see an "invasion" in the evening of what we called "sausage-flies" because of their appearance like daddy-longlegs but about 25 mm long and 5 mm diameter. We would sit outside on the terrace and play cards by the reflected light from inside or visit one another's houses to play monopoly and Colonel Croft even tried to teach us mah-jongg which he had learned in Malaya... The sausage-flies would die over night and be swept out next morning. However, some local people would collect them in basins placed under their lights and cook them to supplement their very starchy diet. They were considered a delicacy but not so the cockroaches that "popped" and splashed all over if you walked on them. Our working day started at 7.00am and we went home at 9.00am for three-quarters of an hour for breakfast after which we returned to the office until 2.30pm. Lunch was followed by siesta, until about 4.00pm after which one pursued one's interests - sport, shopping or whatever until dinner.

Because of the heat and humidity we rose and retired early each day. Buildings were designed to allow for cross-ventilation for comfort as we did not have air-conditioning, only large ceiling fans in the rooms. Indeed, air-conditioning was not really necessary for ten months of the year but would have been very welcome in the month prior to the rains. During that period the humidity increased to unpleasant coastal levels. Clouds appeared on the horizon and increased from day to day until finally the heavy air would become frantic, swirling dust and debris around until the rains burst in streams over the dry laterite which could not cope with the volume falling. The rain washed the humidity out of the air giving a very comfortable atmosphere for a few days until the next build-up of humidity. The cycle repeated in increasing waves until the rain was continuous for about three weeks at its wettest. The cycle then reversed and repeated in diminishing waves until we were back in the dry season. Sometimes there would be some freak rain in December followed by the driest part of the year when the harmattan arrived. This was a cooler wind from the North carrying sand and dust from the Sahara, which even reached the coast some years. This was a very dry air which carried considerable static so that one frequently got an electric shock when touching metal, like the handle of the car. With the rains too the land would burst into life and vegetation would appear spontaneously. Flowers like the desert rose sprouted suddenly from the bark of the baobab tree.

The working offices were accessed from an open verandah and they too had large fans centrally in the ceiling. Outside the door of each office sat a messenger, whose job was to respond to any call from the office, carry files, and deliver letters or messages to another office. Our messenger, Mammah, was a grand old Hausa-man, retired from the army where he had fought with the West African Regiment of the British army during the Second World War. I always found the colonial habit of enrolling local peoples into their armies very disconcerting. War seemed very important to the British, they erected cannons as monuments, regimental flags in churches and peoples were judged by their ability to fight. I used to look at our messenger occasionally and wonder if he knew whom he had been fighting and why.

The Permanent Secretary of the Ministry was a Mr. Jones, a big Welshman called Jonah with a loud voice and devoted to rugby. It was said that at one time when the Sardauna of Sokoto as Minister of Works, was passing along the ground floor verandah, he heard the Perm-Sec. bellowing upstairs and inquired if there was a problem. His aid informed him that the Perm-Sec. was on to Lagos to which the Sardauna responded "why doesn't he use the phone".

There was a hierarchy to the life of the expatriates als, which carried over from that of the colonial administration. On our first tour we were allocated a third floor apartment in a new block, Gwari Crescent, out on the edge of town overlooking Rimi village. From the balcony we looked across the savannah and watched the cow-fulani walk their herds of cattle, sheep and goats across the bush for pasture, going south in the dry season and north during the rains giving a simple rhythm to their life in Africa.

On our second tour we were allocated a first floor apartment in Surame Court, closer to the social center and on our third tour, by which time I had received promotion in the Ministry, we were given a bungalow about 500 meters from the Club.

The house at number1 Ibrahim Zaki Road was small and rectangular with a corrugated iron pitched roof. On the compound we had a kitchen outbuilding, a thatched roofed garage and separate staff quarters for steward and gardener. The site was in an older part of the Government Residential Area and had some fine mature planting including eucalyptus, flamboyant and frangi-pani trees. The avenue was of red laterite and as was expected we put our nameplate just inside the entrance culvert.

1 Ibrahim Zaki Way

Kaduna Club

Socially it seemed we had arrived.

The early 1960s were good years in Nigeria with work and travel throughout the Northern Region which stretched from Sokoto in the Northwest to Makurdi in the Southeast and Ilorin in the Southwest to Maiduguri in the Northeast - about 1,000 km square. I worked in the health division of the Ministry of Works and over the next five years we designed and supervised the completion of a new general hospital in Kaduna and a number of new cottage hospitals from Malumfashi to Jalingo to Suleija as well as miscellaneous clinics and schools. For the first couple of years, one would only meet Europeans driving on the roads and if one met an African driver, it was something to remark "that was an African driver".

My first building was an eye clinic attached to the new hospital in Kaduna. The clinic was financed by Guinness of Dublin brewing fame who had opened a brewery in Lagos. To get advice on the requirements for the operating theatre lamp, I visited an ophthalmic surgeon at the University College Hospital in Ibadan and he suggested I attend an eye operation with him. It was not what I had in mind and felt very uncomfortable to say the least.

Eighteen months after our arrival I met the former Colonial Secretary who had processed my appointment to Nigeria when as Lord Boyd and married to one of the Guinness family he officially opened the clinic on behalf of Guinness.

Guinness Eye Clinic Kaduna Hospital 1961

Some sites such as that at Jalingo were nearly 1000 km from Kaduna and on occasions we made site inspections by air. We would leave Kaduna early and the system was that when we reached the town, we would circle the District Officer's house until we saw him leave by car for the airstrip. We landed and following a coffee snack, he took us to the building site where we had a site meeting with the contractor. We would then go on to lunch after which we were taken to the airstrip and returned to Kaduna, flying around any tropical storms on the way.

On another site visit by road we stopped near Kafanchan in the bush to get some photographs of villagers in the hills but the residents resented our intrusion and we departed quickly. We were up beyond Bauchi another time and came upon a local tribe where the women wore plates inserted to form a greatly extended lower lip. They also wore heavy earrings which stretched their lobes to their shoulders but this was considered a feature of beauty.

Of course as an architect I was asked to assist with the design of buildings for friends in the missions. One such building was a house for the Archbishop of Kaduna. Dr. McCarthy was a delightful person with numerous stories of his early days in Nigeria. They did not have motorcars in the 1930s and cycled from place to place at night to avoid the heat of the day. On one occasion he almost hit a lion which was crossing the road and it was difficult to know which was the more frightened as the lion ran off. He told too of one of his first sermons in a local language. He thought he was doing well until he noted the congregation quietly leaving the temporary hall. He was naturally very disappointed until one of the last departing men pointed to a large mamba in the rafters above him.

Archbishop McCarthy 'cutting the sod'

Archbishop's House Kaduna 1965

Working conditions and housing accommodation were good with standard furniture supplied by the Ministry of Works to all expatriates. My starting salary was one thousand and twenty pounds sterling, rising by annual increments to one thousand six hundred and sixty two pounds. This was a wonderful increase from the six hundred pounds annual salary

I had left in Ireland. My contract included passages to and from Nigeria, clothing and touring equipment allowances as well as quarters at a minimum rent for my family. We received one week home-leave for each resident month and tours of duty were generally from 18 to 24 months. The only leave requirement was that we must depart the tropical malarial world. Such long paid leave was a great bonus and gave a wonderful opportunity for adventurous travel. Trips were planned meticulously over many months. It was the custom if one wished to retain one's steward on return to give him half-pay for the leave period. They usually took the opportunity then to go back to their home area but some would stay on and get another job for the period. It was usual to give them a reference and some of these could be quite amusing. One such reference given by an excited departing officer to an obviously indifferent steward read "If Ali does you as much as he did me, he will be doing very well for himself". Ali presented this proudly when seeking employment.

After my first tour, Dympna and I left Nigeria in October 1961 with 18 weeks holiday plus two weeks traveling time. We took 10 weeks to get home in ten separate flights, stopping off in Khartoum, Cairo, Jerusalem, Beirut, Istanbul, Athens, Rome and London. At that time the Old City of Jerusalem and the West Bank of Palestine had been part of the Hashemite Kingdom of Jordan since April 1950. We stayed in the Old City in a Franciscan guest house called Casa Nova and in the morning woke to the crowing of cocks which had such significance. The Old City Bazaar was like an Aladdin's cave full of craftsmen. There we met a silversmith who showed us a model of an enamel and precious stone medallion he had recently produced for the King to give to President Kennedy as a gift to mark his visit to the USA.

Regretfully the Palestinians said they felt they were treated as second-class citizens by Jordan but then Israel later invaded Palestine in 1967 and by the end of the century the plight of the Palestinians was a sorry state. Sadly the plight of Christians too throughout the Middle East is a sorry tale of hatred and dispossession by Muslims and Jews as told by William Dalrymple in his learned book "From the Holy Mountain".

Photos, typical of the West Bank, Palestine, 1961 and 2014

We did 23 months tour the second time and left with a total of 25 weeks of leave. This time we took the car and went by boat to the Canary Islands for a week and then on to Spain where we crisscrossed both Spain and Portugal for about eight weeks. We reached Paris for the Easter Ceremonies at Notre Dame and when we got to Ireland, I still had so much leave left that I took a job in Dublin for a time.

Northern Nigeria was a Moslem State so we became very accustomed to their close association of all activities to God, to the sense of urgency attached to "Inshallah" and to hearing the muezzin call the faithful to prayer five times each day at which the Moslem staff in the Ministry would withdraw for a short while to pray as they bobbed up and down on their prayer-mats.

Expatriates and Nigerians did not mix much socially in the north as Moslem wives were in purdah and the men did not enjoy a drink culture although both did join together at games. A person's colour was never a problem in Nigeria either. Even during colonial times whites were not allowed to own land so there were no settlers as such. We were employed on contract and could be sent home at any time so we were no threat to the people. Dympna taught in a secondary school and did not see colour but only personality. She often remarked on the similarity of pupils' mannerisms with those of her previous school classmates.Expatriates usually employed a steward and gardener and accommodation was provided to the end of the compound. Each family had two rooms and they shared communal kitchen and toilets. One occasion, Simon our steward rushed in to announce that his pregnant wife was just going into labor. Afraid that she would start delivering in the car, we rushed her and him to the general hospital we had only recently completed, by-passed the normal channels and took her straight to maternity. That evening, Simon arrived to prepare dinner with a grin from ear to ear and the good news that his wife had given birth to a healthy baby boy shortly after we had left them. Next morning she was back pounding cassava for their daily meal, proudly carrying her new child on her back in the traditional manner.

On another occasion a different steward Pius came to borrow 10 pounds, the "bride price" he needed to acquire a wife. The arrangement agreed was that he would repay the loan through small weekly deductions from his wages so he was able to go ahead. However, she never arrived and we never learned what went wrong between Pius and her father.

Six months after our arrival, we took part with all Nigerians in the Independence celebrations of October 1-1960. As expatriate government officers we were invited to the receptions at which Princess Alexandra from Britain, representing the Queen together with the Sultan of Sokoto and the Northern Premier, Alhaji Sir Amadu Bello officially marked the transfer of sovereignty. It was an occasion for celebration and there was a great sense of optimism about the country for the future. As the most populous country in Africa, led by politicians widely applauded for their long experience in government administrations, possessing an efficient civil service and endowed with a strong diversified economy, Nigeria was clearly marked out as one of the major emerging African powers of the twentieth century.

Nigeria's subsequent progress was both assisted and hindered by the discovery of oil. Oil exploration began in 1908 but it was not until 1956 that the first commercial oil discovery was made in the Niger Delta. A series of oil and gas exploration successes then created huge wealth and development. Regretfully this wonderful opportunity gave rise to a 'ménage a trois' of wealth, power and corruption which was at the heart of Nigeria's growing pains.

HRH Princess Alexandra, Lugard Hall

Guests at the Official Reception

DEPARTURE FROM NIGERIA

The Federal Government was a coalition of the conservative northern Moslem Hausa and Fulani peoples and the more radical eastern Christian Ibo, led by the northern moderate Alhaji Sir Abubakar Tafawa Balewa as Prime Minister. The western Yoruba people had the role of "loyal" opposition in the traditional British manner so that to outward appearances, Nigeria presented the promising example of a carefully balanced parliamentary democracy. The problem, of course, was that this idyllic setting was only a mirage, a pragmatic invention which proved unreal and unworkable even in the short-term. Behind this reassuring facade, politicians on all sides were engaged in a struggle for power and profit, conducted in time with such reckless abandon that it led to the collapse of civilian government in six years. Political office at all levels was used by many to accumulate empires of wealth so that politics quickly degenerated to a corrupt and bitter struggle for the spoils of office. The people, of course, became disillusioned and this in turn led to a civil war in 1967, bloody military coups, counter-coups, death and destruction and almost the break-up of the country over the following 40 years. Nigeria has paid a high price for the greed of its leaders which has turned the country from the dreams of the 1960s, where there was very little small-scale crime, into the lawless, corrupt and violent society it became.

The mirage lasted for a few years and the First Republic was declared in 1963 after which time the economy started to deteriorate and by 1965 one began to sense tension in the air when shopping in the market. We departed from Nigeria in 1965 and I was not to return until 1984.
We are hoarders so after five and a half years we traveled home by boat with eleven crates of luggage. The crates were made in the MOW joinery yard in the best of local mahogany, lightly nailed, so on our arrival we had the crates made into beautiful shelving units.

Architectural staff Ministry of Works Kaduna 1965
Cullearn, Ellwood, Graham, Baker, Shemu, Ola, Gulwell, Bowman, Thompson, Nweke, Aje, Waziri, Mitchel, Eila & Bilewu

The first military coup occurred on January 4-1966, with the killing of 18 of the most senior non-Eastern officers and the 3 Premiers of the Federal, Northern and Western Regions. The revolt failed and the army assumed power with General Ironsi as Head of State by popular acclaim. However, he misjudged the political cross-currents and his decision to abolish the regional governments in favor of a unitary state brought riots and the near secession of the Northern Region. He was assassinated some months later and Lt-Colonel Y Gowon became Supreme Commander.

This "Northern coup" was not accepted in the East and a massacre of eastern communities in the North followed. The Eastern Region then announced their secession and Lt-Colonel Ojukwu declared an independent Biafra. A tragic civil war followed from 1967-70. The secession failed too and it was to General Gowon's credit that he made every effort at a peaceful reconciliation with the return of the Eastern Region to the Federation.

The new administration was bedeviled by charges of large-scale corruption and General Gowon was replaced by General Murtala Muhammed in 1975.Some months later he too was assassinated in an abortive coup and General Obasanjo became Head of State, promising to return the country to civilian government. Elections were held in 1979 and the Second Republic was born with Alhaji Shagari as President. The subsequent election in 1983 was considered corrupt so the army again assumed power and General Buhari became President.

Sadly the antipathy between army and politicians continued so that by the end of the century, Nigeria experienced three further army coups and two elected civilian Administrations. By that time too it had become a Federal Republic of 36 States.

The massacre of the Ibos in the North and the Biafran War put great stress on the Irish missionaries. In the North the parishes hid and protected those in danger and passed them on at night southwards from parish to parish while the missionaries held their positions. In the south the situation was more difficult and the missionaries had to retreat with the people as the war progressed. Accordingly, the Holy Ghost Order became fully identified with the "rebels" so the missionaries were expelled from Nigeria when the Federal Army won.

ESB District Office Galway

Communication Building, Tuam

Primary School, Galway

Secondary School, Castlerea

New Churches, Galway and Maree

After our return to Ireland, Michael Quaid and I commenced our architectural practice in Galway in 1968. Some of the many buildings we carried out together, over the next 30 years, are shown above.

By 1975, However, I began to look again for opportunities overseas. Luck was with me and because of my experience in Africa, I became a

Consultant Architect to both the World Bank, Washington DC, UNESCO, Paris and the ADBs for Health and Education projects in the Developing World of Africa and Asia.

SOUTH-EAST ASIA

SAUDI ARABIA en route

First, on my way to the Philippines in mid-1995 I stopped off in Riyadh for almost 2-weeks. I found Saudi Arabia quite unlike anywhere else. John Gunther in his "Inside Asia" saidin the 1940s it was one of the few truly independent states in Asia. I had also heard it later characterized as "an open-air prison" so I did not know what to expect. However, I had thought it very strange that the foreign soldiers who fought in the Gulf War to protect the Saudi state in 1991 were not allowed to take, their personal religious prayer-books or sacramentals with them.

Saudi Arabia, which consists of most of the Arabian Desert peninsula, had not sought a tourist industry and derived its importance as the place of origin of the Koran and the message of Islam. Ibn Saud, who became King in 1925, married some 120 wives, had several scores of sons and numerous daughters. The Law of the Prophet permits 4 wives at a time so the King, who was very religious, married the wives seriatim so he never had more than 4 at any one time. When a wife bore a child she returned to her native oasis or village, where she became a proud ornament to the community. Gunther said that when the King traveled, he took 3-wives with him so that there was always room for a fourth maiden who might catch his royal eye. He viewed marriage as an instrument of unification and in later life stated "in my youth and manhood, I made a nation, now in my declining years I make men for its population". It is amazing to think that oil, now their chief resource was only the secondary objective of an investigation in 1938, made primarily to find artesian water supplies. By 1970 it had become the largest exporter of oil in the world.

Riyadh, until the 1950s was a cluster of monochromatic plastered mud-brick buildings surrounded by date tree gardens. It has since expanded rapidly in grid form to it's present population of one million. The modern kingdom is the result of persistent efforts of the House of Saud to create an unified Islamic State, which they named Saudi Arabia in 1932. Sharia Law dominates and the Islamic religion is very strictly enforced. Alcohol is banned and no other religion is allowed to practice in the country. Expatriates live in their company compounds or enclaves where life can be more relaxed provided it is lived discreetly.

The World Bank developed close relations with Saudi Arabia through a Technical Cooperation Program and while Saudi has a high per capita income and it's social and economic indicators are on a par with OECD members, it often faces problems similar to developing countries. It then turns to the Bank for neutral assessment and advice as part of the Bank's non-lending services. It was in this context that this mission was to conduct the fieldwork for a Public School Facilities Maintenance Study. The Government, as the major provider of education, started in 1947 with 65 institutions and about 10,000 students and by 1990 the system had expanded to about 20,000 schools with an enrollment of over 3 million pupils. Such rapid growth in construction and maintenance requirements presented serious problems and the Bank was asked to advise. Buildings age and deteriorate much as the human body with predictable ailments occurring at the various stages of life so longer or shortened life spans can depend on daily care, nutrition and periodic checkups. Roofs, services, finishes and equipment all have predictable life spans and countries are encouraged to prepare deterioration curves for buildings in their own particular climatic and other conditions. For example a building costing 10 million if un-maintained may have to be replaced in 30 years so that the lifetime cost over 60 years is 20 million. The same building properly maintained annually may cost 13 million over the same period. We reviewed different approaches from voluntary participation and handyman contracts to district maintenance centers. The Ministry of Education was responsible for male schools while there was a separate General Presidency for Girls Education. As part of our work we visited quite a number of very fine schools of both types in the Riyadh district, boys' schools in the morning and girls' schools in the afternoon but only after they had finished and the girls had gone home. Traditionally Saudi Arabia is a male dominated society in which a man's personal and family honor depends on the conduct of the females under his care. Saudi men wear a jellaba, long white gown or thaub and women wear a black outer cloak or abaya and veil. Women are veiled to all men outside the family and they may not board an aircraft or stay in an hotel without the written permission of a male relative. Morals-police armed with camel prods, publicly shame anyone offending their sense of propriety. Although well educated, relatively few women have entered the labor market, perhaps 14% and usually only in fields where they will not come in contact with men. On the other hand, shops and boutiques have all the latest fashions of leading designers and in reply to my query, my companion from the ministry said that the clothes worn in the houses, week-end villas in the desert and when traveling overseas were the haute couture of the world.

As I was a golfer and my mission leader was new to the game and so very enthusiastic, he invited me to join him and his diplomatic colleagues to play. We went out at daybreak to the Riyadh Green Golf Club in the desert, we carried small green plastic mats on which we placed the ball for each shot, blue stakes indicated "water hazard", yellow stakes a penalty area, red stakes "ground under repair" and of course, the greens were brown: a novel experience.

This was my only visit to Saudi Arabia and not getting outside the city, I did not get to know the country. Attendance at public sessions of punishment on Fridays by foreigners was not encouraged and I never even established the protocol for selecting the color of keffiyeh or headdress, white or red checkered, to be worn each day. It seemed to me that at any meeting, the chairman and VIPs wore white while everyone else had checkered but the positions seemed relative because those in checkered today might be in white tomorrow.

HONG KONG

In 1992 I was delighted to be invited to join a Preparation Mission for an Urban Health and Nutrition Project in the Philippines by Stan Scheyer, one of the World Bank Task Managers, with whom I had previously worked in Nigeria.

SE Asia covers an area from the Indian sub-continent to Australia. There are no large landmasses but rather a series of archipelagoes, all of which with the exception of Thailand were colonized by European nations. In the early 20th century most of both Africa and Asia made up the colonial world. Such seemed the natural order to the colonizers and the colonized seemed inseparable until the outbreak of the Second World War. Asia too was seen by the expatriates as more developed and culturally advanced so that it was considered easier to adjust to a transfer from Africa to Asia rather than the reverse.

I was to become very familiar with Hong Kong over the next six years through numerous 2-3 day stopovers en-route to SE Asia. Arriving invariably on weekends by air to Kai Tek airport was always a wonderful experience as one seemed to float down over the busy harbour and between high-rise apartments and offices, seeing the staff working inside, to the runway reclaimed from the sea. It was always a relief when the airplane stopped short of the water. Outside the terminal building to the left, an airport bus service took about 20 minutes to the hotels on Nathan Road at the southern tip of Tsimshatsui, Kowloon.

Following the disgraceful opium wars, Hong Kong was first ceded to Britain in 1842 but hostilities continued and in 1898 China granted the adjoining New Territories to Britain on a 99 year lease. As a resultall of Hong Kong reverted to the Peoples Republic of China at midnight on June 30-1997.

Over the years I was to visit all the tourist sights from Hong Kong Island to the New Territories hilltop lookout at Lok Ma Chau for views over the Shenzhen River and paddy fields to the Peoples Republic of China, which stimulated future visits to the PRC itself over the next few years.

A one-hour trip by jet-foil across the Pearl River estuary took us to Macau, a Chinese Territory under Portuguese Administration. Quieter than Hong Kong and known as the "Latin Orient", it has a Portuguese character in its architecture and churches but with an abundance of casinos, it acquired a flamboyant night-life.

Hong Kong harbor must be one of the most beautiful sights at night but my favorite walk was to cross on Star Ferry from Kowloon to Hong Kong island on Sunday morning when there was little traffic and stroll up through the center, past the distinctive Bank of China, to the Botanical Gardens for lunch or alternatively take the tram to the Peak for the spectacular views of the harbour. In the center too I first encountered large numbers of Filipinos, at about one hundred thousand they were the largest single foreign national resident group and it seemed that most of them congregate in Statue Square on Sunday morning after Mass to meet their friends and exchange the gossip from home. It all sounded so very similar to the Irish of old in New York, behaving like all enforced emigrant peoples. Later in the afternoon I would depart from Kai Tek for Ninoy Aquino International Airport, Manila.

THE PHILIPPINES

Forty eight hours after leaving Nigeria, Manila Airport bore little
resemblance Lagos where every entry and exit could be a nerve-racking
adventure. While awaiting departure from Lagos that March 1992, a
Catholic priest arrived in the last minutes explaining he had driven from
Ibadan, been stopped by bandits, robbed of money, air-tickets, passport
and luggage before being allowed to proceed to Lagos where a colleague
gave him some clothes and money and brought him to the airport to
confirm his identity and experience. British Airways accepted his story as
not unusual and took him to London from where I assume he talked his
way home successfully.

Manila Airport, on the other hand, was bright, open and friendly and
there was a colourful band welcoming in the arrivals hall. The main foyer
was well appointed with banks, taxi counters, courtesy buses and tourist
information desks. In time I was to realise that was the key difference,
countries that seek or encourage a tourist industry make arrival,
departure and visa requirements simple. The ride from the airport to the
hotel, the Manila Hotel where General Douglas MacArthur had made his
Headquarters during the Second World War in Asia, was my first
introduction to the volume, noise and chaos of Manila traffic with which I
was to become very familiar. Traffic there is frequently gridlocked and
many Manilenyo can spend 4 to 5 hours commuting daily.
My impressions of the Filipinos themselves were confused because while
the people were obviously Asian, like Malays and Indonesians, all around
me felt like a State of the USA. Informality was the general rule and
even at government level nicknames were the norm, "Bing", "Chit" and a
senior doctor specialist in public health was simply "Bambi". Few knew
their actual names. A recent President was just "erap" (buddy) to all.
Subsequently I was to learn that they got their religion of colorfully
dressed statues, fiestas and joyful processions from Spain which led one

writer to characterise the Filipinos as a people who had spent 'four hundred years in a Spanish convent followed by forty years in Hollywood'.

Airplane leaves Kai Tak Airport, Hong Kong - Report writing at ADB Manila 1993

Amidst this amalgam of cultures it took me some time to get to know the country and people as a warm and hospitable adaptation of the many influences. I also came to admire the way they could cope with the variety of adversities thrust upon them without loosing their charm and sense of humor.

The Philippines was named after King Philip II of Spain who colonised the Archipelago in the late 16th century and converted the peoples, excluding the strongly Muslim regions of Mindanao and Sulu, to Catholicism. The execution of hero Jose Rizal in 1896 sparked a major revolt for independence and led in 1902 to the exchange of Spanish for American colonialism. The latter then set out to convert the Filipinos to the American way of life. The Japanese occupied the country from 1941 to 1944 and after the Second World War the Philippines became an Independent Nation in 1946. However, both Spanish and US American periods have left deep impressions on the Philippine culture, economy and the country was divided administratively into districts or barangays, named after the large boats of their Spanish past.

The Philippine Archipelago is made up of over 7,000 diverse land units from small coral reefs to large tropical islands with palm trees and golden beaches stretching over 2,000 km between the Equator and Tropic of

Cancer. Politically it is a democracy, modeled on the US American pattern but has experienced some turbulent periods.

One such period of dictatorship and marshal law ended in 1986 with a wonderful example of "people power" displayed in a four-day bloodless revolution by the people when, responding to the call of Jaime Cardinal Sin, literally hundreds of thousands with the combined leaders of Politics, Church and Army rebels, marched on the Epifanio de los Santos Avenue EDSA and saw the widow of the assassinated Benigno Aquino installed as President. Ten years later the Far Eastern Economic Review was to say that the EDSA revolt had the impact of a political Pinatubo, referring to the volcano and was a watershed in inspiring revolution against unjust dictatorial regimes around the world. People Power was subsequently used with success to remove President Joseph Estrada.

In 2001 the Nobel Peace Prize Award, the first of its kind given to a nation by the Nobel Foundation was awarded to the Philippines by Pierre Marchand of France of the Nobel Peace Prize Laureates Foundation, with the words:

"The world salutes the Filipinos for their courage in overthrowing two undesirable Presidents. You have given the gift of effecting radical change without firing a shot, in a world that only knows force and violence. The legacy of people power would be the Filipino peoples' gift to the world. You were given a national gift, do not keep it to yourselves. The world will never be the same again if the spirit of EDSA prevails beyond the shores of this tiny archipelago".

In 2001 also the Global Non-Violence Award was given to the 70 million Filipinos, the first recipient of this award given by the Center for Global Non-Violence and Lou Ann Guanson, vice president of the Center said:

"We agreed to grant the award in recognition of the non-violent struggle of the Filipino people as exemplified in EDSA People Power which was done twice in this country."

At the beginning of the 1970s, incomes in the Philippines were at levels comparable with Korea and Taiwan but during the 1980s their average growth was over 6% while the Philippines grew at less than 1%. Growth did no more than trickle down to the majority so that a combination of slow growth and economic and political crises during the 1980s left the Philippines in 1992 with a real per capita income 7.2% lower than in 1980. Similarly, while Health and Nutrition conditions had improved since the early 1970s, progress had been far slower than other East Asian countries. As a result, the Philippines infant mortality rate which was comparable to those of China and Thailand in the 1970s was by 1992 roughly twice their rates. Similarly their social indicator levels for life expectancy at birth, infant mortality, child malnutrition and illiteracy were only about midway between the developing and the developed worlds.

The Project we were to prepare with the Department of Health, an Urban Health and Nutrition Improvement Plan, was to directly address poverty alleviation by improving the health and nutrition status of the slum dwellers in the 21 urban areas of the National Capital Region NCR of Metro Manila, Metro Cebu and Cagayan de Oro. The goal of the project was to provide basic services to people in these areas in order to allow them manage and control resources available to them as well as participate in governmental and non-governmental interventions. The project was to be implemented by the Department of Health which at that time was led by the popular and flamboyant Health Secretary Juan Flavier. The primary health care program included family planning and the public debate in the media on the means to be used, between the colorful Minister and the statesman Jaime Cardinal Sin became legendary.

Every DOH week started about 9am Mondays with all the staff lining-up in front of the Department for a pep-talk by the Minister. He would encourage them to greater achievements and he ended always with "lets doh it" to wild applause.

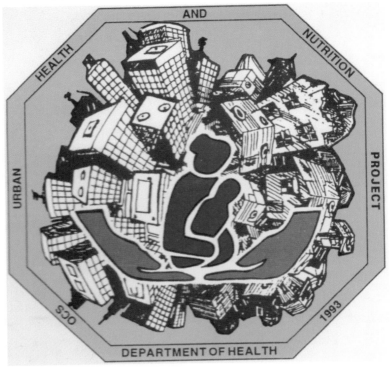

UHNP Project Logo

Lack of affordable housing had spawned squalid and teeming slum colonies, veritable rat holes of death and disease and the NCR contained the bulk of urban slum dwellers and accounted for 4.6 million or 87% of the urban poor in the 21 project areas. They were ravaged by illness and disease that resulted from and aggravated by overcrowding, filth, dirty water and unsanitary toilet facilities. Worst hit were the women and children, females in the reproductive age group and pre-school children so the particular sector identified by the project as needing immediate servicing were those women and children's group i.e. the majority of the slum population.

Under the service delivery component the project aimed to provide health centers in the selected areas complete with new equipment, furniture, drugs, food supplements, micro nutrients as well as ensuring adequate personnel and training. My input related to the civil works sub-component of the service delivery by evaluating and implementing the rehabilitation of all the facilities necessary, including new buildings where required, to achieve the project objectives. This, of course, meant that I had to travel considerably throughout the project areas and I was to get to know all 21 urban areas very well over the following five years

For the project facilities, we promoted the principles of good-design for the desired comfort levels in the tropical zone without unnecessary mechanical means, which meant proper orientation, planned sun-shading, natural light and cross-ventilation over work spaces. The project office itself however, closed all windows, pulled curtains, turned on all electric lighting and air-conditioners and excluded all contact with the outside world. I enquired a number of times as to the reason for this unusual behaviour and although "external noise" was tentatively suggested, I suspect that the exclusions were more related to the principles of a branch of Chinese thought known as feng shui, which seeks to site all building elements harmoniously in natural surroundings. In addition, the toilets never functioned properly during my years visiting the DOH.

The major problems in Manila at that time were the notorious "brownouts" when electricity might be off for hours. I arrived during a midday brownout at one deep-planned city health office with staff workspace far removed from any possible natural light or ventilation. It was impossible for the staff to continue working so everybody was just sent home.

I really enjoyed working in the Philippines although meetings in the Department Project Office itself always seemed to be a struggle against chaos. Meetings were an experience since they were being constantly interrupted. They would be just settling down when a young man or girl would enter whom you might recognize as someone you thought was a junior messenger around the place. The chairman would stop the meeting to give the entrant their full attention. This might go on for some time during which all around the table would break into individual discussion groups. The meeting resumed after some time and progress was being made until suddenly it was time for merienda. Plates of rice cakes, bibingka, fish or meat in sinigang and many other tasty dishes would arrive with tea, coffee or calamansi.

Slum community, Manila 1992Boys' circumcision "coming of age"

While it was indeed very hospitable of them to go to such trouble for us, it was always a great relief for me to break away with the civil works people on field-trips to building sites and facilities.

During our inspections I might make suggestions for construction or planning improvements but nobody seemed to take any notes.

Accordingly, at the end of the day when we had finished, I would get with them around a table, maybe over a beer and write the minutes of all we had decided. I would copy and distribute the minutes next day or maybe even include them in my final report.

At the beginning of the 20th century Manila was a small Spanish-style city of churches, hospitals, schools and public buildings. It was built on the

Pasig river, much of it below sea level and subject to frequent flooding. It was devastated during the bitter fighting of the Second World War but with independence in 1946 the rebuilding began. By the 1990s the NCR had become a large con-urbanisation of some 10 million inhabitants spread over seven cities: Manila, Quezon, Caloocan, Makati, Mandaluyong, Pasay and Muntinlupa and ten municipalities: Navotas, Valenzuella, Malabon, San Juan, Marikina, Pasig, Pateros, Taguig, Paranaque and Las Pinas. Some of these were upgraded to city status by the end of the century.

METRO MANILA – NCR

The NCR stretches about 30 km along the large natural Harbour and 20 km inland to the mountains and Laguna lake. For such a mega-city the infrastructure is grossly inadequate, it's traffic jams notorious and commuters can spend up to six hours in daily travel. Metro Manila is a city of enormous contrasts, exclusive expensive clubs and housing estates of mansions for the very wealthy, with securely guarded entrances like that at Forbes Park in Makati City to the densely populated housing for the poor of Tondo in Manila City or the fishing area of Navotas Municipality in the North-West. We had to specify the floor levels of the health clinics to be 1.2 meters above the level of the roads because they could be covered with up to one meter of water at high tide. Such flooding presents great difficulties when trying to provide a clean potable water supply, adequate soil and waste disposal and prompts the question of one writer "how many poor men does it take to make one rich one".

Worse still were the slum dwellings scattered widely and particularly along the mud banks of the Pasig River which bisects the NCR. Pollution is also a major concern and one sees many people in some streets wearing their handkerchiefs as breathing masks. It was in Manila too that I first became aware of 'noise' as a serious pollutant. Large volumes of screeching vehicles were constant, even when one awoke in the middle of the night. Quezon City is more open with middle class estates, municipal and other clubs, large hospital and the University of the Philippines. Tourism is centered round the old walled Intramuros, night-life in Ermita and Malate to the business high-rise area of Makati City and, of course, one of the delights of an archipelago in those latitudes is the abundance of sea-food available in restaurants all over.

Each year I got around to all cities and districts with colleagues of the Department of Health Infrastructure Division and met some wonderful and interesting people like architects Luis Ferrer and Chito Gahol. We would set off early making site visits all day with "pit-stops" at one of the abundant American-style fast-food joints like "Jolliebee", a place where one eats rather than dines. Traffic delays could be whiled away reading the large coloured hand painted billboards advertising current movies which are a feature of the streetscape. I arrived at an outpatients' clinic on one occasion to see young boys queuing cheerfully to be circumcised and as each was done the next would jump up on the table for his turn. It represented 'coming of age'.

On another occasion, selecting sites for clinics in Mandaluyong City, I was accompanied by the Mayor who took us proudly to lunch at the Wack-Wack Golf and Country Club. He told me that his father had come to Manila from northern Luzon Island while he was just a baby. His father had got a job as one of the green-keepers in the Wack-Wack Club so the future Mayor grew up as a caddy to players in the club. Today he was justly proud that he was not only a single handicap golfer but a distinguished member of the club and a powerful Mayor of the City.

In one municipality, Las Pinas to the south, the District Health Officer invited me to visit his house where I was to discover that he was an accomplished woodcarver and sculptor and that as a hobby he was breeding beautiful fighting cocks for what is a very popular sport in the Philippines. In Las Pinas also I called to see the famous Bamboo Organ in the Parish Church, built by a Father Diego Ceva in the early 19th century. It had recently returned from Germany where it had been renewed and tuned and it was delightful to arrive for a Mass at which it was being played.

From there it was a short journey to the Taal volcano filled with the lake Taal from which emerges a smaller volcano inside of which is a smaller lake. The views from the volcano ridge at Tagaytay were spectacular and well worth the trip for Sunday lunch. During the day-trips and stops at the many fast food outlets for lunch, I got to know the architects and engineers, their way of life and their concerns. I discovered people are much the same everywhere but economics, environment and governance make us different.

It was generally unsafe to enter the slum districts unless one was accompanied by a person known and trusted by the inhabitants so I was taken each time by the local midwife. Such visits had a salutary effect and made me very grateful I was born into what by comparison are very privileged circumstances. Living conditions were appalling and even surviving in those slums was itself a struggle so it was heartbreaking to learn that even at that level, life is controlled by corruption. The single standing water hand-pump maybe one hundred meters away was "owned" by a mafia who charge a few centavos for each small bucket-full.

Traveling to another deprived area I stopped off to see the infamous Smoky Mountain, the vast notorious dump continuously smoldering on which poor urchins scavenge for anything they might be able to sell. Happily Smoky Mountain was removed during land reclamation and development improvements in the mid-1990s.

Occasionally at the end of a field-trip and to avoid the worst of the peak traffic for others I would make my way from the Department of Health to the hotel using the Light Rail Transport LRT to San Isidoro and then by the uniquely Filipino public trans'jeepney' for the experience.

The LRT is an overhead rail system which can be a very pleasant off-peak ride over the city although it darkened and destroyed the streets on which it was routed. The jeepney, on the other hand in all the cities, is essentially a lengthened army jeep with benches on the sides to hold about twelve people, painted every color of the rainbow and decorated with innumerable badges, lights, horns, mirrors, tassels, maybe animals or birds on the hood, probably a picture of the Virgin Mary on the dashboard and a tape-deck blaring rock music all the way, they are incredibly cheap and popular but not for the fainthearted as they do not appear to obey any rule.

CEBU

Cebu the tourist center of the Philippines, famous for guitars and poignant ballads, is situated on a shell-like necklace of islands known as the Visayas to the south. Cebu's most famous historical landmark is a wooden cross planted by Ferdinand Magellan in 1521 to commemorate the celebration of the first Catholic Mass in the Philippines. Here too is the venerated shrine of the Santo Nino, a 300 millimeter high statue of the Christ Child, given by Magellan as a baptismal present to Queen Juana of the Visayas who said it would replace the idols of the people and is the oldest relic of the country. The Lapu-Lapu monument on Mactan Island nearby commemorates the battle, reenacted annually, where Magellan was slain by the native chieftan Lapu-Lapu.
Metro Cebu, composed of the cities of Cebu, Mandaue and Lapu-Lapu, rejoiced in an economic boom, the downside of which were a proliferation of slum colonies in the three cities where they numbered over half a million or 50% of their entire population. Progress invariably inflates land values and the cost of construction so that housing for all was not possible. In these circumstances for want of shelter, the migrants built what passes for houses on any space when no-one is looking and the result was that of the populations in 1994, 55% of Cebu, 51% of

Mandaue and 50% of Lapu-Lapu wallowed in slums. At the opposite end of the social scale there is the internationally known Shangri-La's Mactan Island Resort, a beautifully landscaped thirteen hectare development by a private beach with six varieties of restaurant cuisine catering for a tropical lifestyle of health, recreational and sport activities which must be one of the leading idyllic retreats in Asia.

Health Office Meeting, Mandaue
Bacolor submerged in Lahar after eruption of Mount Pinatubo 1991

We visited one slum area raised on stilts over the mud banks which we negotiated on duck-boards. The the mission leader Althea Hill made contact with one of the women and learned that the family had recently lost a baby from a diarrhea infection even though the infection could have been easily cured and the slum was only about one kilometer from an health clinic. It was a profound example of the importance of the health awareness programs of the project.

The direct benefits of the project to nearly a million households in the three target cities would include better access to health and nutrition services, reductions in infant and maternal mortality, advice on the spacing of births, elimination of vitamin A deficiency, reduction in protein-energy malnutrition, anemia, goiter, incidence of pneumonia and the prevalence of tuberculosis

I visited all the barangay districts of Metro Cebu from Guadalupe to Talamban and from Gun-Ob to Suba-Basbas on Mactan Island as well as to the island villages, one such was Pangan-An a small island of two hundred people which was being considered for a small outpatients clinic under the project. The island is less than one meter above sea-level and we went out to it by banca, a small motorized outrigger.

Our first mission trip to Cebu was particularly memorable because after our arrival an air-controllers strike started so we obtained tickets for a return trip by boat. However, the ferry was heavily booked, took over twenty four hours and did not have a goodrecord for punctuality, not to mind safety in those shark infested waters. Accordingly, the mission leader chartered a small airplane to take the eight of us back to Manila after asking each of us if we were agreeable to fly in the circumstances. In reply to our query about our chances of landing in Manila given the air-controllers strike, the pilot replied that he was happy to fly in the belief that anything that went up must come down! As we enjoyed the beautiful one and a half hour flight over the islands at something over 2,000 meters, I had to pinch myself to make sure I was not dreaming and was actually being paid during this delightful trip.

This mission chartered an airplane to get back to Manila 1992

In time the uniqueness of that trip took on a special significance for us and became a test of memory to list the eight people present on the flight: 3 Americans, 2 Filipinos, 1 Japan, 1 German and 1 Irish. Cathie, Chris, Stan, Dodong, Luis, Aki, Petra, Author

CAGAYAN-DE-ORO

The third city of the project was Cagayan de Oro, a fast-developing urban center in Mindanao and although the number of slum dwellers was relatively small, was chosen for the project to serve as a test case in arresting budding urban decay at the sapling stage. An old legend tells us that the name Cagayan is derived from the word Kagay-haan which connotes "shame". This legend dating back to the 16th century relates that a Manobo tribe living in Kalambagohan was attacked by another tribe from a nearby mountain. The beaten villagers planned to retaliate but before they could, their own chief fell in love with the daughter of the enemy chief and married her. Because of this the Manobos were disgusted and renamed their place "Kagayhaan" meaning place of shame. The Spanish changed this to Cagayan and when gold was found in the local river "de Oro" was added.

Cagayan de Oro is located along Macajalar Bay on the central coast of northern Mindanao, the second largest island in the south of the Philippines. It serves as the regional center and with forty urban and forty rural barangays has a population of nearly half a million.

I was able to inspect nearly all the facilities in the twenty barangay districts of the project from Patag, where I found an Irish Columban Fathers' mission house, Catanico famous for it's falls and rapids, Camaman-An, Lapasan and Macabalan where General MacArthur landed by PT boat on his way to Australia after escaping from Corregador during World War II.

I was unable to get to the health station at Besigan as the road was impassable during the rainy season but was able to visit a beautiful thatched roofed conference center on the coast at Initao which is a favorite spot for project workshops. An hour further south passed Iligan

City we had an opportunity to visit the Maria Christina Falls, one of the earliest projects of the Asian Development Bank, where the sight of the fifty eight meter straight cascade from the observation platform at the hydroelectric station was spectacular.

We were taken to see the housing and hospital facilities at the Del Monte Plantation about ten kilometers south of the city and we went out into the farm where pineapples stretched as far as the eye could see in all directions. We seemed to end all field-trips at different seafood restaurants often dining on a cantilevered platform over the beach. Throughout all my fieldtrips to the health facilities, I never ceased to be impressed by the devotion and care of the nurses who in spite of sometimes the greatest of difficulties were always cheerful and immaculately dressed. I was not surprisedthen in the late 1990s when the Ireland Minister of Health visited Manila to recruit the first 70 Philippine nurses to work in the hospitals.

It is not possible to think of the Philippines in the 1990s without being aware of the terrifying earthquake which occurred at 4.26pm on July 16-1990. The epicenter was at Cabanatuan but was so powerful at 7.7 on the Richter scale that it rocked the Capital, 90 km to the south. Similarly, the violent eruption of Mount Pinatubo on the 15 June 1991 killed many and caused havoc, covering large areas with incredible amounts of lahar which continued to sweep down with the rains to greater depths for many years afterwards. The project architect James Cochon took me to the town of Bacolor where his aunt had lived and it was eerie to drive on hardened lahar, now a couple of meters deep, where one could only see the rooftop of the house where she had lived. The town monument was buried and only the head of the central statue protruded above ground. We also walked straight in through the rose window to the choir gallery level of the parish church. The place was truly dead except as a tourist attraction.

The Filipinos were heroic before their fall, as guerrillas during the Japanese occupation and again later with the American army in the eventual liberation of the Philippines. They suffered greatly throughout the Second World War so one Sunday afternoon Cathie Fogle and I sailed out to Corregidor Island at the mouth of Manila Harbor which was the site of the US-Filipino last stand in 1941 against the invading Japanese army. It is now a National Shrine run by the army where the ruins of the mile-long barracks, General MacArthur's headquarters in the Malinta Tunnel, the Pacific War Memorial and a museum give a thought provoking insight into the history of that time.

Model: "I have returned" Gen McArthur in the Visayas 1945

After one of the Philippine missions and already halfway, I decided to continue around the world by the Pacific and the United States. We stopped at Seoul and even though we were only in-transit, we were obliged to leave the airplane with our hand-luggage and come back through an intense security again. The perceived threat of North Korea had never before impinged on my world.

We continued on to San Francisco where I spent a delightful week-end. I stayed at the St. Francis, took a tram to Fisherman's Wharf where I enjoyed a chowder in a scooped-out spherical bread-roll, visited the Maritime Museum USS Pampanito and in the evening, returned to the top of the Mark for a sundowner. Next day I walked across the Golden Gate Bridge, took a bus to Muir Woods, spent some time in a "clear well-lighted place for books" and in the Theatre in the Square in the evening.

VIET NAM

I was absolutely delighted to join a mission to Vietnam for my next project. Vietnam, which means the Viet people of the South, evokes many emotions and conjures up images of war so far away. I suppose we all see it only as it touches our imagination personally. From Ireland one sees the similarities; colonized, oppressed and partitioned leading to a long struggle to eventually win freedom, unity and recognition. The Viet were a race known since antiquity as a migratory, hunting people that came south from China. I don't think it is possible to understand the Vietnamese or to work there successfully without knowing something of their recent past. Over time they have had to defend themselves against the Chinese, Khmers, Chams, Japanese, French and the USA.
Stanley Karnow's "Vietnam" is probably the definitive history and begins aptly with a quotation from the Roman historian
Tacitus: *"they made a wasteland and called it peace".*
The following is a short chronology of the major events of the 19th and 20th centuries:
1802   Vietnam unified by Gia Long
1833   Nguyen Emperor signed treaty making Vietnam a Protectorate of France
1887   France forms Indochinese Union of Tonkin, Annam, Cochinchina & Cambodia

1919   Ho Chi Minh petitioned the peace conference at Versailles for Vietnam independence but without success

1940   Japan occupies Indochina

1945   Japan capitulates and the WWII in Asia ended August1945

The War in Europe was straightforward in that Hitler invaded independent nations so that anyone helping him must be an enemy of freedom. In Asia, Japan's claim to be liberating *"Asia for Asians"* was accepted initially by many patriots including Sukarno in Indonesia, Roxas in the Philippines and Aung San in Burma as freeing their nations from colonial rule and many collaborated at the beginning. However, the Japanese proved to be worse tormentors than the masters they drove out and by 1945 most Asians were glad to have their old masters back, or so it seemed. In fact the whole region had changed utterly, in the words of Lee Kuan Yew "my colleagues....had emerged determined that no one had the right to push and kick us around. There was never a chance of the colonial system being recreated. Scales had fallen from our eyes and we saw that local people could run the country".

It had seemed the war was over but to millions of Asians, devastated by the clash of empires and drained by colonial rule, the fighting had just begun. The occupation of Indochina by Japan during the war had demonstrated the fragility of the Western domination over South East Asia in general and over Vietnam in particular. In Indochina, Japan handed over power to Ho Chi Minh's Vietminh who declared independence and set up a Provisional Government in Hanoi before the French government returned.

1946   France accepted the "Free State" of Vietnam within the   French Union.

1954   France defeated in the battle of Dienbienphu

        Geneva agreement incorporates partition of Vietnam

1955   First USA aid to government of South Vietnam

1959 North Vietnamese begin infiltrating the South using the Ho Chi Minh Trail

1962 US Military Assistance Command formed in South Vietnam

1963 Vietcong defeat South Vietnamese, 15,000 US troop advisers

1965 Vietcong attack US installations, US troops reach 200,000. President Johnson authorizes US bombing of North Vietnam

1966 President De Gaulle visits Cambodia and calls on USA to withdraw. US troops reach 400,000 by year-end

1968 Tet-counter offensive. US troop levels reach 540,000
The war continued for the next five years with the bombing of Cambodia, North Vietnam and HCM Trail through Laos.

1973 Cease-fire agreement reached in Paris
The last US troops leave in March

1974 North Vietnam continue the war against the South

1975 Saigon is captured and the last US marines leave the US Embassy in Saigon and Vietnam is unified.
The Khymer Rouge under Pol Pot take-over in Cambodia

1978 Vietnam invades Cambodia and relations with China deteriorate. US recognition of Vietnam postponed

1979 The Khmer Rouge deposed
China retaliates with a short invasion of Vietnam

1989 Vietnam leaves Cambodia

1991 Communism collapses in the USSR and Russian aid to Vietnam ceases

1992 President Mitterant visits Vietnam and normalizes relations with France

1994 President Reagan lifts the US embargo in February.

Vietnam seemed the perfect illustration of the expression;

"The strength of the weak lies in their ability to absorb suffering while the weakness of the strong lies in their disproportionate use of violence which in the end destroys them"

The multi-national organizations responded immediately and my first visit to Vietnam was three months later as part of a World Bank mission to prepare a Family Health Project. Over the following fifteen months, I was to participate in the preparation of three projects in health and education so I had to travel extensively throughout the country. Vietnamese embassies were few and far between so on my first trip I had to stop off in Bangkok to obtain the necessary visa before proceeding to Hanoi and the Dan Chu Hotel. Dan Chu means Democracy and it was a wonderful old five storey French colonial building with open verandahs on Pho Trang Tien in the center of the city near the old town between the Municipal Theatre and the Hoan Kiem Lake. It was popular with visiting groups and one morning we noted five different multinational project missions at breakfast. Someone at our table queried in passing, prophetically as it happened, that with all this Western development influence, how long Hanoi would retain its easy friendly style? Within a decade friends from home visited Hanoi to find it greatly changed; population, building density and motor traffic had all greatly increased leading to a nosy and aggressive environment in which petty crime had become normal.

There were only two of us on the first mission, we met in the hotel and over the next few days met the Government personnel at the Ministries of Health, Education and Construction to plan the mission program. I then set off by air with Ho Anh, who was to be my companion and friend on the field trips. Ho Chi Minh City, the former Saigon.From there we drove south about five hours to Cao Lanh which we used as a base for visiting health facilities in Dong Thap Province. This is a remote Province on the Mekong River Delta, a vast rice growing region and is intersected by a dense network of watercourses where the land is often flooded during the rainy season. We wished to see a sample cross-section of the two hundred health centers in the Province ranging from Commune to District to Provincial level facilities.

Fieldtrip with Ho Anh Vietnam   *Mission in Hanoi*

People in isolated areas were served by mobile health stations often aboard a boat which could duplicate as a maternity ward or propaganda office when necessary for awareness programs. Travel was not easy and health agents traveled by moped or boat and on a subsequent field-trip, I had the wonderful experience of spending one day on a motorboat visiting isolated facilities on the delta watercourses in flood.

Water pollution was a major problem where more than 90% of the population did not have clean water so UNICEF carried out a program of drilling wells with hand-pumps.

We returned to HCM City and from there we flew to Danang. The trip by the coast road to Hue is a beautiful two-hour drive and we stopped about halfway at a restaurant, sitting out on an headland with spectacular views of the South China Sea. Ho Anh advised me on the fresh fish soups, seafood, crustaceans and nuoc cham dipping sauce, used to such delight with cha gio, small rolls of minced pork, prawn, crab, mushrooms and vegetables wrapped in a thin rice paper and deep-fried until crisp. The restaurant was run by four sisters and we were invited into the open kitchen to enjoy the act of preparing the meal where food presents such an important social occasion. Vietnam has a cuisine culture influenced by China but with a more fresh herbs and all the spices they can grow, to give a distinct subtle flavor. It has been helped too by the later influence of French cuisine with baguettes, pate and spring rolls.

Located in the center of Vietnam, Hue was for a long time the historic capital and probably no other region has been more influenced by China in what used to be called Annam. Hue was the center of the Nguyen Dynasty and the tombs of their Emperors along the Perfume River together with the Thieu Mo Pagoda landmark are among the most precious monuments of the city. At the center stands The Imperial City, built on the same principles as The Forbidden City in Beijing and commenced by Gia Long in 1804. It has suffered over the years from French shelling, internal revolution, typhoons, thieves and finally US destruction during the tet offensive. We stayed at the very distinctively decorated Huong Giang Hotel overlooking the Perfume River while we were visiting the health facilities in Thua Thien-Hue Province, one of a string of coastal provinces along the center where the width of the country reduces to 50 to 60 kilometers.

We returned to Hanoi to learn that my mission colleague had been recalled to Washington DC and I was to continue the civil works evaluation for the Government alone. I was to become very familiar with and very fond of Hanoi over the mission periods, so much so that my wife Dympna joined me there for a holiday at the end of one mission. Hanoi was a pedestrians' city and for exercise we liked to walk from the hotel around Hoan Kiem Lake. North of the lake is the old town, a maze of tiny by-ways and twisting covered lanes full of shops or stalls, called the '36 Streets district'. It is the traditional soul of the city also known as the Ancient Quarter. There you can see elderly women with lacquered teeth blackened by years of chewing betel and young women wandering about in traditional ao dai, the beautiful white or pastel colored robe and pants synonymous with Vietnam. It is very elegant attire sometimes unfairly referred to as the garment that covers everything but hides almost nothing.

The stalls are open to the street with kitchen behind and living quarters upstairs. The area is a living community of all ages and everyone has their place. Women ride in from the market gardens on their bicycles with fresh produce and minor intersections become mini-markets. The whole area is a treasure chest where one can find virtually anything in the numerous stalls and shops. Dympna, an enthusiastic craft-shopper loved it.

It was possible to walk from the hotel to the Ministries, lakes and parks but sitting comfortably in the front of a cyclo, a tricycle with a double seat in front, became my favorite means of transport to work, restaurant or tours in spite of the sometimes nerve-wracking manoeuvring through the multitude of traffic. The water puppet theatre by the lake too is a traditional form of entertainment unique to Vietnam. Hanoi is a beautiful city of lakes, parks and tree-lined avenues, traditional and French colonial building including the Municipal Theatre or Opera House which the French undertook to restore and upgrade in 1996.

However, Hanoi was changing rapidly, at first bicycles dominated but in the 15 months of my visits, mopeds and smaller motorbikes started to take over and cars increased. The noise levels too increased: at first pretty silent but with mopeds the air became filled with the "beep-beep" which was magnified with the motorcar.

Architecturally, change was all around and in spite of a policy of keeping low-rise construction in the central area buildings began to creep-up in size and density thereby raising traffic levels. However, it was blessed with an abundance of good restaurants serving traditional and French cuisine like the Indochine on Nam Ngu Street to the Cha Ca in the old town and many more specializing in the local barbecued fish and minced fish meat cakes.

One evening I happened to be in the company of 5 vegetarian Indian Nationals, all on missions and when they suggested we go out to dinner, I said I'd join them later for coffee. I went to 'Le Loft' for "an entrecote and wine and was then delighted to join them.

My regular 'cyclo' in Hanoi 1995   *Site visits by speedboat on the Mekong*

From Hanoi we could visit the health centers of Bac Thai, a mountainous province to the north where Ho Chi Minh set up his base in the hills for safety and to plan the liberation struggle. It was in the provincial town of Thai Nguyen that I first heard the loudspeakers continuously ringing out the party achievements of the industrial factories and agricultural production on the collective farms which Ho Anh translated for me, with some embarrassment I thought.

From my inspections of facilities throughout Vietnam it was clear that due to the wars, isolation and economic constraints over the previous decades there had been little upkeep of the building stock with consequent deterioration of infrastructure leading inevitably to considerable under-utilization of the health center services.

It was intended that the first phase of the project would provide support to about twelve hundred facilities in five provinces representing the north, center and south. The process required the setting up of surveys to establish exactly what services and facilities did exist, their condition in respect of staff, medicines, equipment, furniture and buildings including utilities, site and development works and locations so that whatever services, if any, did exist could be mapped, quantified and evaluated.

The first preparation mission of any project is essentially fact-finding and tries to agree a work-plan of surveys for the accurate collection of all the necessary data and should also agree accommodation models for each of the services to be provided in the project so that firm proposals can be prepared and priced. Plans for future maintenance and sustainability of all the elements must also be incorporated in the project document. This stage is normally done using private consultants or government staff but in Vietnam, a communist country where there was no private sector and department staff had been run down due to lack of finance, they had to improvise. The expertise, of course, exists but in the command economies, where there was no such thing as competitive bidding, it is not available in the format we know in the West.

I talked to the Project Manager of the need to find a suitable architect or engineer to carry out the necessary surveys, design proposals, specifications and costs. He got an engineer but we felt that, while we would keep him in mind for the implementation, we needed someone capable of doing quick sketches with a 6B pencil rather than a 4H, as we distinguish architects from engineers in the business. However, an architect was found in the University Architectural School who together with his colleagues in the school formed a "private practice" to undertake the work.

The outcome was very successful professionally but a little sad otherwise for a time because the architect who was well paid, I understand, was overwhelmed by the relatively large sum of money to cover his colleagues costs and expenses. When I arrived on the next mission, apparently he had disappeared, left home, did not pay his colleagues and the Revenue Department were looking after him for tax. It was suggested by the Project Manager that if he was found and failed to discharge his liabilities, he could be jailed and Rama delightedly suggested the possibility of me too since I had interviewed and recommended him. In time, the whole issue was resolved satisfactorily and the episode became a good story.

Although my responsibility related solely to the civil works component I decided, since I was alone on that first mission, to try to set surveys in motion for subsequent disciplines. I remember asking myself what my friend Stan Scheyer would look for if he were here so I instigated surveys of the Primary Health Care and Nutrition programs provided together with their current lists of drugs, instruments, equipment, stocks and staff at each facility.

The second mission, which ideally takes place when all the above is completed, tests the accuracy of the information thus far and continues to the detailed design and costing of the project.

Such projects in which I was involved were usually implemented over five years during which time it was reviewed at the half-way stage and evaluated on completion in order to establish if the project did actually achieve its objectives and to what degree of success so that both sides could learn from any shortcomings before preparing the next phase or project.

The next province visited was Hai Hung, another great rice producing region, east of Hanoi in the Red River Delta and famous for its orchards of lychee. The following mission went south again to HCM City in order to visit other areas of Dong Thap Province and the Mekong Delta. The former 'Saigon' was the Capital of South Vietnam 1954 to 1976. HCM was very different to Hanoi, the largest city and river port with a population of nearly five million,retains a strong French influence in its architecture and churches. It is the business capital and has absorbed western culture to a much greater degree under the influence of the United States. It is a vast commercial area; a mini-Bangkok but with street muggers and prostitutes on mopeds.

In all the economic indicators: per capita GNP, incomes and material living standards, it was ahead of Hanoi but comparing the social indicators; healthcare, education literacy, child malnutrition and infant mortality, the north was ahead which was an interesting reflection on the priorities of the two influencing cultures.

We drove from HCM city north-east for some seven hours over hills of wonderful green vegetables and fertile valleys to the beautiful mountain resort Dalat, provincial capital of Lam Dong in the south central highlands and home of many minority peoples. Its more temperate climate made it a favorite retreat of the Emperor Boa Dai and the French from the heat of the coast and the bustle of Saigon. Dalat has many churches and the stained glass windows in the Cathedral were brought from Grenoble, France. The Project Director Dr.Cuong came with us from Hanoi on this field-trip and we were treated to dinner there by some of his friends. Later the first evening I went for a walk around the main streets near the hotel to feel the ambiance of the town and I was to learn later that Dr Cuong, who obviously felt a responsibility for each of his foreign charges, had followed keeping about fifty meters behind on the other side of the street until I was safely back to the Hai Son hotel.

As well as our inspections, we always took every opportunity to visit tourist sights when convenient including the Prenn Waterfall and on the way back one evening, I suggested as a golfer that we should see the new championship Pine Lake Golf Club. I went over to talk to the two men putting the finishing touches to the 18th green to find that one of them was Australian and the other Irish, both working for the Singapore building company that had the contract. I noted that individual membership of the club was open at USD 12,000 entry fee plus USD 600 subscription which included use of the clubhouse and swimming pool and qualified use of the health club. Vietnam was changing fast. Returning to HCM City from Dalat we descended about 1500 meters through forest to the Boa Loc plateau of tea plantations and noted for the breeding of silkworms.

We returned again to Hanoi for a day or two for meetings and the review of mission progress before we set off again, this time for Son La Province in the north-west close to the Laos border to inspect both schools and health buildings. Son La is a mountainous province about 300 km from Hanoi and its population of 800,000 includes twelve minority peoples including Thai, Hmong, Kinh and Lao so it has a patchwork of different dress, customs and practices.

The highlands are very fertile with an abundance of tea, coffee, mulberry and fruit and on the way we first passed Muong villages where the people were noted for their colorful dress before rising to the Moc Chau area of tea plantations and dairy farming. Farther on we came to the beautifully terraced rice fields of Yen Chau. We stayed at the Hoa Bin Hotel in Son La and the local authority invited the visiting group to a dinner followed by traditional dancing and a sing-song with a difference. There was a large jar or calabash of a local wine put in the center and all men and women were given a long, say 1,500 meters, thin bamboo - the idea being that we put one end in the jar and sucked the alcohol as we danced around the jar. The dance ended when the jar was empty and I remember wondering what and how strong the local brew was because as a guest one had to participate. It was all very enjoyable and I felt very privileged that they had gone to such trouble to put on such a wonderful display of their local culture.

Next we visited Quang Ninh Province on the coast to the north-east bordering China. We stayed at Hong Gai, which although less that 150 km from Hanoi took about five hours by car. The busy road east passed the paddy fields of the Red River Delta to the major port city of Hai Phong. On the way we crossed a long single lane bridge shared with the railway which had priority. There were also two ferry crossings which had to be negotiated. At the end of our work the project committee presented us with beautifully sculptured
pieces in anthracite. The major attraction of the province is Halong Bay, with its spectacular limestone islands rising like sculptures.

I returned to Halong Bay again on holiday with Dympna.
There are over 3,000 islands, inlets and rock outcrops and we spent an afternoon on the bay, stopping off to see the vegetation covered islands

and grottos of stalagmites. Once we got from our boat to a smaller sampan in order to go through a low arch in a rock outcrop to an inland sea surrounded by tall sheer cliffs which reminded me of the French film "Indochine". In the silence we could hear the birds singing in the still air. On the way back we met a family of five, parents and three children, selling coral shells from their 6 meter boat, on which they lived, cooked and earned their living. However, just to sail the clear crystal turquoise waters among the limestone spires, the junks and sampans with their distinctive red sails gliding-by adds to the tranquility and timeless serenity of the experience.

Health Officers and colleagues, Halong Bay 1995

Contrary to preconceived images fashioned during the years of wars, the Vietnamese proved to be a very gentle and friendly people in a beautiful landscape from the paddy fields of the deltas with children riding water buffalo, to the sculptured rice terraces and plantations of the highlands. 80% of the people are engaged in agriculture making Vietnam the third largest exporter of rice after the USA and Thailand.

While we were there too, the Minister's mother died so Althea, Rama and I went to the house. The family was there and friends called to pray by the corpse. They sat around the room having a drink, talking about and listening to the experiences people had in relation to her life and her end. It was just like a wake at home, quite unlike our experience in Bali Indonesia some years earlier. There a man who was highly respected in the village died but he was not wealthy and could not afford a cremation ceremony. He was embalmed and preserved for a couple of months until a wealthy man subsequently died. Both bodies were then cremated in one combined ceremony paid for by the wealthy family. The ceremony was advertised and attended by many and became a tourist event. We filed past the corpse laid out on the bed and then waited outside until it was carried out and placed in a large timber coffin shaped like a bull to indicate his wealth. The funeral set off and was joined at the first intersection by the other simpler coffin and continued as a single funeral festival to an open area, prepared in advance for the cremation. The decorated catafalques, 3 to 4 meters in height, were tilted precariously to pass under electricity and telephone wires on the way. On their arrival at the appointed place, both coffins were placed together on the decorated platform and the bonfire was lit amid the great excitement and joy of the large attendance. It was all over in about 15 minutes.

Working in Vietnam was a wonderful experience. Meetings were orderly and productive and on each subsequent visit, one could see the fruits of the earlier missions. From my time there, I would expect Vietnam to become a leading light of the SE Asia region in the 21st century. My colleague Bengt Jacobson, architect from Sweden, took over the supervision of the project and I went on to prepare another similar project in Cambodia. I was sorry when my work in Vietnam was finishedin 1996 but before going to Cambodia, Dympna and I set off for our long planned holiday in China.

PEOPLES REPUBLIC OF CHINA

The last Emperor of the Qing Dynasty PuYi came to the throne in 1908 aged 3 years. The early decades of the 20th century were troubled with a series of civil wars between the various warlords. The 1917 October revolution in Russia greatly influenced the spread of socialist ideas and led to the formation of the Communist Partyin China. In 1931 the Japanese occupied Manchuria and installed a puppet government led by PuYi but it was overthrown in 1949 when the Peoples Republic of China was formed by Mao Zedong. China became a Communist State almost the size of Europe and virtually closed to foreigners. It has 56 nationalities and about one third of the world's population. Serious internal conflicts continued in an effort to remove the remaining feudal rulers and separatists' campaigns continued in Xinjiang and Tibet. A revolution in 1989 in Tiananmen Square Beijing with students demanding greater democratic reforms was brutally suppressed. However, China is now changing very fast and its development may prove to be of major significance in the 21st century.

I had been to Beijing in 1994 when travelling home from the Philippines. I had first planned a stop-over in Tokyo but the mission team suggested I would see little there over a weekendand a glass of beer cost 15 $ so I changed my routing and my short visit to Beijing was planned like a military operation. I left Manila at 35*C and arrived via Hong Kong next morning to-5*C without an heavy coat. Mary the guest relations manager at Novotel had sent a taxi to meet me and the driver, Mong, had an extra anorak for me. Since few I would meet understood English, she had sent a page of helpful instructions in English and Chinese characters so that I could select my preferences and direct Mong accordingly. He only understood the Chinese characters and was highly amused by the system. It worked perfectly and we set off for Badaling about 70 km to the north. The Great Wall, built by successive Emperors

2,500 years ago as a fortification against invaders from the north, is about 5,000 km in length with watchtowers every 250 meters or so. It stretches along mountain ridges and can be seen from outer space. It is an impressive sight, particularly near Badaling, where it had been restored to its eight meter height and six meter width. We returned by the Ming Tombs and Memorials, where 13 of the 16 Emperors are buried, to see the famous stone figures and Ding Ling Museum of many rare relics. We returned to Tiananmen Square by 7pm to see the changing of the guard at the Mao Zedong Mausoleum before arriving at the hotel to a dinner of Peking Duck. The ducks are specially fed to ensure the crispy finish and it was served complete with all the side dishes.

Early next morning Mong was on-hand to take me to The Forbidden City, the distinctive group of Imperial Palaces of the Ming and Qing Dynasties. The layout conforms to feudal etiquette with ancestors to the east side, gods to the west, government buildings to the front and living accommodation behind. The three Big Halls - Supreme Harmony, Complete Harmony and Preserving Harmony - provided the foundation of China's Imperial Power from where Emperors assumed their reign. The many buildings and courtyards symmetrically grouped on either side of the central axis, had overhanging yellow roofs, red walls and the attention given to the distinctive decoration and detailing make it a rich architectural experience and joy to behold.Mong met me two hours later at the rear in Jingshan Park and took me back to the hotel. He later took me to the airport for afternoon flights via Hong Kong to London.

My return with Dympna in 1995 was a much more leisurely affair with plenty of time to enjoy the sights properly. Of particular note this time were the Temple of Heaven and the Summer Palace on Lake Kumning. The Temple complex is laid out to the needs of a sacred ceremony because it is believed to be the only place on earth with direct access to Heaven for the Emperors who were regarded as celestial go-betweens.

The main building, the Hall of Prayer for Good Harvests, has become the symbol of Beijing.

The Summer Palace, 20 km from the city, was used by the Emperors and their court as a retreat from the heat of the capital for 800 years. It has been restored so that today with the Lake, Temple of the Fragrance of Buddha, Marble Boat, Bridge of Seventeen Arches and the beautiful Jade Belt Bridge, the area is a wonderful park-land retreat for everybody.

On the way to the palace we stopped at the zoo to see the pandas. We expected the place to be very quiet at 9.30am but found a long queue at the zoo entrance. China had a one-child family policy and the queue was largely made-up of grand-parents taking their grand-child, almost always a boy, to the zoo while their parents worked. Foreigners do not have to queue but can go straight in but pay a much higher entrance fee.

The Forbidden City, Beijing, China 1995

China was largely closed to foreigners until recent years. Its size and diversity are so immense and varied that we were anxious to see something of the interior so shortly after our arrival at the hotel, we called to the tourist desk to see if we could do a trip on the Yangtze River. We were aware that the famous 'Three Gorges' would soon disappear with the completion of the Sanxia Dam.

Next day the tourist lady had a proposal so after discussing it with the French Manager of the hotel, who saw no real problem provide we accepted that all trips in China were an adventure, we accepted. Two days later we flew to Chongqing, known as the mountain city in the eastern part of Sichuan Province where we stayed in the Chung King Hotel in the city center and a short walk from the Chaotianmen wharf on the river. The airport seemed quite a distance from the city in a mountainous area because as we came in to land the ground was close one minute and quite a distance the next. The area, known as the furnace of China, was rough country so we were taken to the city by a 4-wheel drive jeep.

Next morning we were collected early and taken to the river, which was low. We had to walk down a long flight of steps and then a distance on timber planks over mud banks to the boat. We noted there was nobody about and the boat was being refitted so was obviously going nowhere. We heard beckoning calls from another boat. We worked out that the second boat was owned by the same company and was doing the trip instead so we were happy to go aboard. Our temporary guide however would not part with our boarding cards because the name on the ticket was different to that of the boat. In time she relented and we were shown to cabin number one. We were the only non-Chinese on board, nobody spoke English and all writing was in Chinese characters so I'm not quite sure even now how all communications were brought to a successful conclusion. The crew used to knock on our doors at mealtime and we were lucky to be able to use chopsticks because there wasn't anything else available. We spent four days on the river to cover 750 km from Chongqing to Wuhan, stopping off to visit the towns and places of interest along the way. It was quite unlike any tour in the western world. The Ghost City of Fengdu was particularly weird to us, we went up by cable-car to a sequence of temples with walks including Ghost Street lined with sculptures of grinding punishments, souls traveling around the underworld, selected gruesome tortures and ending at the Temple of the King of Hell.

On the second day, two Chinese men from Singapore who joined the cruise were delighted to talk English so they "adopted" us and advised on all aspects of the trip from food to tours and turned out to be great companions.

The Changjiang / Yangtze River, flowingwest to east and navigable for 2,500 km to Shanghai has been China's major transportation route for 2,000 years and a quarter of the country's agricultural land lies in its vicinity. All quays are floating type because flooding has always been a terrible problem giving rise to thousands of deaths each year. The new Sanxia Dam is intended to control the water flow and thereby avoid the human tragedies. Scenically the most beautiful section is the 200 km stretch from Fengjie to Yichang which includes the Three Gorges: Qutang is 8 km long where the river is only 100 meters wide with sides rising from 500 to 1,000 meters high, Wuxia is 40 km and Xiling 80 kmlong.

Fengdu on the Changjiang River- Sichuan Province

Our tour also included the lesser but very spectacular Three Gorges on the Daning River, the largest tributary which joins the Yangtze near Wushan. There we got into smaller boats for this trip of 50 km which included riding shallow rapids with the crew guiding the boat with long poles. Sheer cliffs rise on either side where coffins can be seen in caves up high which were used for burials in the past.

With lush vegetation, bamboo trees, waterfall and animals, the stretch which includes the Dragon-Gate, Misty and Emerald Gorges has been designated one of the key nature reserves in China. The boat did not go the full distance because apparently the previous day a number of Taiwanese tourists were drowned. We notedlife jackets were not issued on these boats.

When we got to Yichang, Hubei Province we were told that the boat was not going any further so we continued our journey by bus to Wuhan. We stayed overnight at the Qing Chuan Hotel on the banks of the Yangtze overlooking the famous Pavilion before flying back to Beijing the next day.

China had been a remarkably thought provoking experience. It was so different that I became conscious of the very different and complimentary influences which generated human behaviour.

European development for 2000 years has been influenced by Christianity which teaches humanity to strive towards perfection in this life and this behaviour will influence our life in the next. Accordingly, it stretched people to greater efforts not only at home in Europe itself but ever further and further overseas in all fields. This has been exemplified in the heights of achievement of European culture in the arts, sciences, communications, commerce and technology and has led to the dominance of Europe in the world over the past centuries.

Asia, the home of the other great world culture, has been influenced by Buddhism which spread from India to China over 2000 years ago. Asia, by contrast, internalised its life approach to seeking harmony in all things of life and environment past, present and to come. China then sought to maintain the integrity of this distinct culture and to exclude or minimise and adapt external influences as far as possible. This objective was largely successful until the explosion of communication in the 20th century and the resultant changes now taking place may prove very significant and have a profound effect on the future in the world in the 21st century.

CAMBODIA

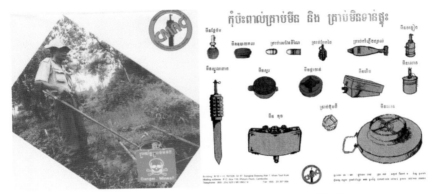

Cambodian Mine Action Centre

Since the demise of the Khmer Empire in the 15th century, Cambodia had really been at the mercy of its larger neighbors, Thailand and Vietnam. Cambodia had been incorporated into the French Indochina Union in 1887 and the country was governed by puppet kings until the Second World War. When Japan occupied all of Indochina, a group of pro-independence Cambodians realized how weak France really was and this marked the beginning of Cambodian Nationalism which led to Independence in 1953.

The period from the 1960s to the 1990s saw a new low for the country so that to the world at large, Cambodia has conjured up images of war and suffering. The reported death of Pol Pot in 1998 and the decision of the Government to bring the remaining leaders of his regime to justice locally again focused attention on the sad history of Cambodia.

One is reminded of the undeclared war euphemistically referred to as the "side-show" 1969 to 1973, during which it suffered over half million tons of bombing by the US, greater than that dropped on either Japan or Vietnam during their respective wars. This bombing at a time when the Khmer Rouge guerrillas were fighting to overthrow the Government, is said to have dehumanised the people and left the country in turmoil. It was followed by the appalling nihilistic depravity of the Khmer Rouge era from 1975 to 1979 during which time the Cambodian people suffered some of the worst human tragedies to afflict any country, in consequence of the Pol Pot policy to return the newly named Kampuchea to "Year Zero".

Within days of their coming to power Brother Number One, as he was called, started the forcible evacuation of Phnom Penh which at that time had a population of two million. The period is well documented in the film "The Killing Fields".

The tragedy was, I thought, palpable on arrival in 1995. I found the Tuol Sleng Prison Museum, the high-school which became the main torture and interrogation center, still retained as it was, more harrowing than the Choeung Ek mass-graves and monument of human skulls and bones on what became known as "the Killing fields" about 15 km from Phnom Penh or even Auschwitz-Birkenau in Poland. The practice of the regime was to photograph each prisoner before their execution and the museum now displays the numbered photographic images around the walls of the former classrooms. Seeing the actual terror in those eyes is frightening.

Cambodia had lost a generation and I remember, even during my first week, being conscious that the society was 'fragile'. People were subdued and even the expatriates seemed tentative and cautious. There wasn't the same vibrant excitement that one found in the Philippines or Vietnam.

The World Bank Atlas of Development indicators showed Cambodia well behind Vietnam and among the poorest countries of the world both economically and socially. I was to work there between 1995 and 1999 and the first two missions of about eight persons from the USA, Britain, Canada, India, France and Ireland were to prepare a Health Development Project.

The six provinces selected for phase one were not only based on density of population and need but also dictated by the security situation in the country at that time. Cambodia suffered from poorly developed official institutions and services as a result of the wars, a depleted human resource base due to the destructive policies of the Khmer Rouge and continuing rural insurgency.

The project focused on a five year effort to assist the government in the reconstruction and expansion of the primary health system with particular emphasis on reducing death and sickness from leading communicable diseases such as tuberculosis, malaria and HIV/Aids.

My function again related to the revitalisation of the facilities required to fulfill the expanded services. Travel was restricted because of sporadic violence and the amount of unexploded ordnance, anti-personnel and anti-tank mines of which a director of the Cambodian Mine Action Center said in 1997 that there were perhaps 10 million buried in the countryside.

For the earlier missions we stayed at the Cambodiana Hotel which was built originally for Prince Sihanouk's guests in the style of the palace but some evenings we would go for a short walk to the very pleasant Red Restaurant for a change. Nearby was the Irish Rover Pub which I visited to meet their clientele, which including aid-workers in the NGOs to learn of conditions in the provinces.

When I returned in 1998 it seemed Phnom Penh had declined and crime increased since my previous visit eighteen months earlier but we stayed at the beautifully refurbished French colonial Royale Hotel under the management of Raffles from Singapore.

Negotiating an improvised bridge, Cambodia 1995

One member of the smaller supervision group, Pierre-Yves Norval had earlier lived in Phnom Penh and knew the city as a resident. On arrival for the mission he hired a moped with sidecar for freedom of mobility and site visits. Occasionally we would get away from the hotel for an alternative menu in a different scene so that careering around Phnom Penh late in the evening in the sidecar is still one of my more exotic memories. Another was to spend some time rummaging through the stalls of the Russian Market off Monivong Street. There one could get almost anything from a needle to an anchor, local crafts, Buddah figures, coke, biros, kitchen utensils, fake Rolex watches and it seemed faked everything. I bought a few Chinese compact discs of Mozart classics and two DVDs of popular films at $ 2.50 each as well as a cd of about $1000s of software packages all for 4.00 US dollars obviously pirated from somewhere of poor quality.

Between 1995 and 1999 we did have an opportunity to inspect many facilities in the Provinces of Kandal, Kampong Speu, Kampot-Kep and Siem Reap as well as around the Capital but found the situation generally depressing. Because of the decades of upheaval and lack of maintenance, buildings were in poor condition. We visited Kampot Province, destroyed in 1975 by the Khmer Rouge and Kompong Som, the former Sihanoukville, which also suffered from the bombing and was due for redevelopment.

The countryside was dotted with Pagodas while Phnom-Penh had a certain French ambiance and was a very pleasant capital on the banks of the Mekong River where there was a riverside promenade to walk by the beautiful Royal Palace and Silver Pagoda. A favorite hostelry was the Foreign Correspondence Club used by those reporting the terrible events of the recent past. It was a pleasure to sit at the open balcony overlooking the meeting of the River Sap with the Mekong while eating a steak in a baguette, that US-French creation "le sandwich".
Going to Mass there was a new experience too as the Church, tabernacle and furniture were in Cambodian style. It had the appearance of a pagoda as one left their shoes at the entrance and sat anywhere on the floor while the priest, a Jesuit from Ireland on one occasion, servers and all sat around the altar during the celebration.

Post-conflict Cambodia was just recovering but judging from the experiences of other traumatised peoples improvement would be slow and this seemed to be accepted by those working in the country. In Ireland for instance the pain of people dying or fleeing famine in the mid-19th century, while Britain was the world's richest empire, still remains in folk memory. Half the population was under 15 years of age and it was fascinating to listen to the few older senior officials tell of how they survived the Pol Pot years by simply fading into the countryside, many working quietly in the fields of the hill-tribes. Any sign of Western education or influence could mean instant death so they discarded everything including their spectacles to achieve anonymity to survive.
It is not surprising then that Cambodia is now probably better known for the 'Killing Fields' than 'The Angkor Temples'. I visited the architectural

and engineering schools in Phnom Penh, where I met two lecturers from Dublin and also the beautiful National Museum, to get a sense of building and design in the country but our visit to Siem Reap and Angkor were especially memorable.

ANGKOR

Dominating the paddy-fields of the Central Plain is Tonle Sap Lake, to the north of which, in a sprawling valley jungle, stands Angkor the ancient Royal Capital of the Khmer Empire, which flourished from the 9th to the 15th century. It was a remarkable city of over 600 temples, palaces and pagodas of which at least a dozen compare in size with the great cathedrals of Europe. Most celebrated of the temples is the early 12th century Angkor Wat, acknowledged to be the most magnificent example of ancient Hindu-Buddhist architecture in the whole of Asia. Here in the province of Siem Reap it is easy to see why the Angkor complex is considered the heart of Asian culture and the land-mass, now Vietnam, Laos and Cambodia, was called Indochina.

Angkor Wat temple
the largest and artistically the most accomplished

However, with the decline of the Khmer Empire, the agricultural system collapsed, the buildings decayed and the royal capital was finally abandoned early in the 15th century. Angkor was consumed by the jungle and virtually lost to the world for over 400 years until it was re-discovered by accident in 1860 by the French naturalist Henri Mouhot. The forgotten city had by then become part of the folk memory and the local people told him that the monuments had been the work of giant gods. Only the temples remained and all the other secular wooden buildings had decayed. The discovery of the lost city in the far-off jungles of French Indochina captured the imagination of Europe and brought archaeologists, adventurers and treasure hunters who have all since taken their toll on the ancient splendours.

Over the years since their discovery, the temples have been subjected to systematic plundering by invading peoples. There are stories of decapitated statuary being bartered on the Thai border and rich collectors ordering 'genuine' treasures of Angkor from display catalogues in Bangkok, the merchants then going to take the items from Angkor for delivery.

In the 20th century, modern archaeology and physical science set about retrieving the ancient capital in order to preserve, what are recognised as some of the world's most impressive monuments, in their wonderful lush tropical setting. This restoration had to be abandoned in the early '70s due to political upheavals but was recommenced in the '90s.

The Angkor complex which stretched 25 km by 10 km encompassed a sophisticated irrigation system with a food growing capacity for one million inhabitants as well as the multitude of buildings in laterite, brick and stone. ANGKOR WAT, which is the largest and artistically the most accomplished of the temples, was designed by the king's architect and built from a wax model by artisans, labourers and slaves. The construction, contemporaneous with Notre Dame in Paris, took 37 years to complete and was dedicated to the Hindu god, Vishnu. It had a network of hidden drainage which probably saved itover time from the excesses of the monsoons so that it is now the best preserved of the monuments.

Angkor Wat covers 80 hectares and is a physical representation of Hindu cosmology. The five central towers, lotus-flower shaped and emblazoned on the national flag, represent the peaks of Mount Meru, the centre of the Hindu universe on whose summit the gods reside. The outer wall represents the mountains at the edge of the world and the 5km surrounding moat, the oceans beyond. The walls of the outer gallery, in circumference about 1km, are covered with sculptures in bas-relief, telling narratives from the stories of Vishnu, Krishna & Rama as well as depicting scenes of the Khmer army in victory.

The Khmer adapted aspects of Hinduism introduced by Indian traders and nearly every surface is richly decorated with stylised motifs including Apsaras-celestial nymphs, Naga-mythical serpent, Garuda-bird-man and Singha-guardian lion.

One of the finest sculptures is the 160 feet long bas-relief that depicts an ancient legend of the creation known as "the churning of the sea of milk" in which the central figure, Vishnu, in a co-operative effort with demons to the left and celestial gods to the right, in a tug-of-war using the serpent, churn the sea from the foam of which springs the food of the gods - immortality.

The BAYON stands at the centre of the largest city of ANGKOR THOM which was the last great temple, dedicated to Buddha and vying with Angkor Wat as the most frequently visited monument. The layout is similar but the bas-reliefs are of Khmer life including their land and sea battles. The special features of the Bayon are the 54 towers, representing a model of the kingdom, each carved with 4 large near-identical heads facing the cardinal directions. The central large tower again represents Vishnu in the churning of the sea and features 4 gigantic heads with the same enigmatic smile.

The south entrance gateway to Angkor Thom straddles the laterite wall and overlooks the moat that surrounds the city. In front, the broad causeway is lined with two rows of giant figures, pulling on enormous nagas, enacting the same scene carved on the Angkor Wat gallery.

Another temple, TA PROHM was built to house the divine image of the Queen Mother. It contained 39 sanctuaries, 566 stone and 288 brick dwellings and functioned as a monastery which was home to 18 abbots and 2,740 monks. According to contemporary inscriptions, the temple required 79,365 people for its upkeep and relied on the income of 3,140 villages. Ta Prohm is of particular interest because it has not yet been cleared of its undergrowth. It is just what you would expect a "lost-temple-in-the-jungle" to look like and illustrates the spectacular effects of forest encroachment. Seeds carried by birds and dropped on the temple roofs, sprout aerial roots that trail to the ground from where they grow and expand between the stones, envelope and ultimately crush the heaviest of stone structures. The French writer Elie Laure wrote of Ta Promh "------ with its millions of knotted limbs, the forest embraces the ruins with a violent love".

Another Temple -Ta Prohm
the jungle took over

There are many other monuments at Angkor, some up to 20km distant and not accessible for security reasons. Today the Khmer people are very proud of their rich heritage and Cambodia has been returned to the tourist brochures, sometimes as part of a Far East package which allows 3 days to include an overnight trip from Phnom Penh to Siem Reap to visit Angkor. Most fly but the more adventurous travel by boat on the Mekong. Architectural schools in the West, study the historic styles from the Middle East, through Egypt, classical Greek, Roman and the middle ages to this century, the progress of which was largely based on the evolving structural capacity of each period. Theyhave influenced modern architecture throughout the world and perhaps this is why in contrast the architectural allegories of Angkor are so enchanting.

BANGKOK

Bangkok, City of Angels, is the easiest access point for Cambodia and Vietnam so I was delighted to take the opportunity to see the city and some of Thailand over the years of my frequent visits to south-east Asia. Bangkok, the International gateway to the Kingdom of Thailand, is a hectic metropolis of five million people with traffic jams which are notorious. Because of the richness of its architecture and the easy charm of the people it is the most popular tourist destination of South-East Asia.

Independent for eight hundred years, Thailand was never colonized although both Britain and France had designs on the territory since it was a buffer between their possessions in the area. At the beginning of the 20th century, Thailand was forced to sign a Treaty granting suzerain rights to both in respect of some border states. However, Thailand did agree a more favorable treaty with them in 1925 and this led to an expansion of their trade with Europe.

Thailand became a pawn of the Japanese during WW II and declared war on the Allies in 1942. In 1946 they signed a peace treaty with the Allies and on their recommendation Thailand became a member of the United Nations.

By the close of the century the economic and social indicators show Thailand as one of the most prosperous countries of Asia with a per capita GNP of about 3000 USD and a life expectancy of 69 years. Lying between the Equator and the Tropic of Cancer with a beautiful climate, Thailand caters for tourists at every level from the wonderful and exotic to the sordid and erotic with all commodities nicely packaged and easily available for every taste. It was here that I first met sex treated openly as just another commodity. Thailand too has become a popular golfing destination and with two beautiful courses convenient to the airport either of which are great for anyone stopping off to adjust to time-lag before a mission without facing the traffic.

The Thais are the direct inheritors of Khmer culture as seen in its architecture so every visit to the Royal Grand Palace with its halls, temples, residences and pavilions is a new experience.The richness of detail, color and decoration in the roofs, wats, monuments and sculptures within the whole complex is a delight.

The spirit of Buddhism prevails in Thailand and is most obvious in the multitude of temples throughout the country. Most residential and commercial compounds include a doll-like spirit house generally set on a post and sited after complex astrological consideration that reminded me of the Chinese principles of fengshui. They can vary from simple wooden units to ornate mini-temples. They are believed to bring good or bad influences depending on the site position selected and are regularly adorned to please the spirits. Elsewhere in Asia, where such a site is deemed sufficiently significant, they may even erect a building or pagoda in order to trap or hold on to the good spirit.

Of the many temples in Bangkok, the Wat Arun across the Chao Phraya River is my favourite not only for its beauty reminiscent of an upper terrace of Angkor Wat but as one of the most prominent monuments. It also offers great views of the Grand Palace, Royal Temples, river and the city. Thai style domestic housing stands on timber stilt framing, a precaution against flooding, with steep roof-tiles, timber floors and carpet squares that it very open and cool. The best examples are in the country but samples from different locations can be seen at the house of the US American, Jim Thompson who revived the silk industry after the Second World War, an industry for which Thailand is justly proud.

The capital Bangkok of course, is not Thailand so I decided to see Ratchaburi and Kanchanaburi Provinces to the west bordering Burma. Thailand is a fertile land and the second largest exporter of rice after the USA. At Damneon Saduak there is a large floating market which is exotic in its produce and the best example of such throughout SE Asia. Every boat is a business, some equipped with primus stoves and supply "take away" meals extraordinarily cheaply. I visited Jeath, the open air War Museum at Bantai Muang and took a train across the infamous Bridge on the River Kwai immortalised in film. "Jeath" replaced the word "Death" and is an anagram of the initials of the nationalities involved; Japan, England, America, Thailand and Holland and is dedicated to peace by showing the terror of war. The bridge was built between 1942 and 1943 by 30,000 prisoners from the above countries and more than 100,000 impressed labor from many Asian countries including China, India, Indonesia, Malaysia and Burma.

Royal Grand Palace, Bangkok Taj mahal India

SOUTH ASIA

BANGLADESH

My first mission for the World Bank was to Bangladesh in 1978. Following my visit to the WB in October 1977, I received a telephone call from Ms Ishrat Hussain at the Bank the following February asking if I was free to participate in a Bank mission for a Health and Population Project in Bangladesh. I accepted and was asked to be in the Intercontinental Hotel in Dhaka on April 12. They helped with the travel and reservation arrangements. Some weeks later I departed for New Delhi, India where I arrived about six o'clock in the following morning. Rest-stops were allowed at that time, of one to two days depending on the length of journey and I arrived at the Oberoi Intercontinental Hote, Zakir Hussain Road.

Following shower, change and breakfast I was at the hotel entrance at 10.00am complete with taxi and guide to set-off for Agra, 200 km to the south. We stopped on the way for lunch and while the guide enthusiastically related the history of Moghul Emperors and their influence on Delhi and Northern India, I concentrated on the new experience of Indian food in India with tanoori, gustaba, kababs, dahi sauce and spices on a foundation of pilau complete with the inevitable chapatti. I was also fascinated at the efforts of a man across the road under a large mango tree settling down comfortably on the back of an elephant, presumably for his siesta.

The main objective of my trip was Shah Jehan's mausoleum for his wife, Empress Mumtaz Mahal, the Taj Mahal and on arrival I left my companions so that I could quietly enjoy the whole visual symmetrical composition which few buildings in the world can rival. I approached the entire composition of mausoleum of brilliant white marble walls broken by deep shadowed arched recesses and topped with the balloon-like dome all framed with four minarets at the corners of the white platform. I passed the long reflecting pool in front lined with evergreen trees which enhance the cool whiteness in a magnificent fashion so that it seems to float above the ground under the clear blue sky.

I arrived back in Delhi in time for an early dinner at the hotel restaurant where we were entertained with a cabaret of classical Indian dancing. Next morning the taxi and guide were on hand to take me to see the sights of Delhi, the old city of the Moghuls built by Shah Jahan who built the Taj. The new city was built in the colonial era, the work of architect Edward Lutyens who also designed Arus an Uachtaran in Dublin the official residence of the President of Ireland, formerly known as the Vice-regal lodge. The showpiece of New Delhi is the Red Fort, the shah's multi-pavilion palace and pearl mosque on the west bank of the Yamuna River.

In that April afternoon I left Delhi airport on a two hour flight to Dhaka in the center of Bangladesh. As the airplane descended, I remember hoping the pilot would find enough dry land on which to land as there seemed to be water everywhere. Of course, we were coming down over the meeting of the Brahmaputra and Ganges Rivers and to the south it seemed to be one vast delta. The annual floods submerge vast areas and the occasional abnormal floods penetrate and inundate most of the country which is predominantly a great flood-plain and deltaic landmass very low and flat. Not surprisingly the Shapla or water lily is the National Emblem.

It was in Bengal in the mid-eighteenth century that Britain made her first successful bid to establish their rule in India which culminated in the British Empire of India by the mid-nineteenth century. We have seen earlier that while the Japanese claim to be liberating Asia for the Asians was initiallysuccessful and accepted by many patriots as freeing the nations from colonial rule, the Second World War had changed everything and gave rise to a determination by subject countries to be one's own master. In the story of Asian liberation Mahatma Gandhi stands out as a beacon of inspiration. The Dalai Lama said of him that he won independence for India by simply telling the truth because his practice of non-violence depended wholly on the power of truth and justice.

In 1947 Britain partitioned India into separate Hindu and Muslim Nations and the new India and Pakistan emerged. The partition of India meant splitting both the Punjab and Bengal states between the two nations. The capital of Punjab, Lahore, went to Pakistan and India engaged the French architect Le Corbusier to design a new capital, Chandigarh, for the Indian Punjab. East Bengal became East Pakistan, over 1,600 km from West Pakistan. Relations between the East and West parts were never easy, a great geographical and cultural divide separated the two and in 1971, backed by India, East Pakistan seceded to become the independent Bangladesh and the subsequent Indo-Pakistan war resulted in victory for India.In 1975 the Bangladesh's independence hero, Sheikh Majibur Rahman, was assassinated and the army assumed power.

When I arrived, the country was coming to the end of the resulting marshal law and the political situation was quite relaxed.

The government in 1977 decided that the population rate of increase had to be curbed substantially if the country was to achieve economic growth and political stability. The first 5-year plan had projected a total population of 189 million by the year 2000 which they considered they could not sustain economically. Accordingly, the Population and Family Planning Division decided they must bring down the number of children born per woman from 6.4 to 2.6, replacement rate by 1985 and maintain an average 1.5% growth rate for the period 1977-2000.

The revised projected total population was then estimated to be 121 million by 2000 and this they considered manageable. They initiated a program of family welfare centers, family planning clinics and training complexes with additional family planning staff in order to implement it. The World Bank supported the Government policy with their Health and Population Project. We were on a double mission so I was to supervise the civil works of the first project and a Sweedish architect,Jean-Erik

Lundeberg wasto prepare the second project. This was great for me on my first assignment and I learnt a lot from the experienced Jean-Erik. Public policies in respect of population control were highly controversial everywhere and while most countries included family planning awareness as a component of maternity and child health of primary health care policy, some treated it in a distinct division or even a separate ministry from health, depending on the fervor of the promoters. Islam did not approve and the Catholic position was stated in the Pope's Encyclical "Humanae Vitae" in 1968. I mentioned the subject to a US American priest there and while he stated the official position, pastorally he was more concerned that the population control policy might be extended to include compulsory abortion or sterilization both of which were popular across the border.

He was an interesting man and had a great love for the people of the country. He was there since 1945, never moved and yet was in three countries; India, Pakistan and Bangladesh. Certainly one became quickly aware of population density and on a field-trip to Tangail, we stopped on a bridge. The river bed below was dry and was being dredged by people carrying basins and buckets of mud on their heads. There were thousands there, I had never seen so many people anywhere and the sight reminded me of an anthill which had been broken years before in Africa exposing innumerable ants moving in all directions.

My abiding memories of downtown Dhaka too were the crowds, the staining on all buildings due to the high levels of humidity, the difficulty in getting around among all the rickshaws and the apparent chaotic tangle of telephone wires hanging unevenly everywhere. I was impressed by the number of Non-Government Organisations working in the country at all levels of emergency and development aid. I had dinner one evening with Father Angus Finnucan, founder of the NGO Concern during which I asked him where they got all the voluntary workers. He replied they were mainly from Ireland and many of the ladies were those that in an earlier generation may have become nuns.

I had to do some traveling outside Dhaka and the countryside was flat and fertile except for the Chittagong Hilltracts in the South and the tea plantations of Sylhet in the North. The people were warm and friendly, poetic and artistic. In 1978, Bangladesh had a per capita GNP of 108 US dollars per year and was one of the poorest nations in the world. It had a life expectancy at birth of 47 years and a school enrollment of 37%. The land area was less than twice that of Ireland or Georgia State in the US while the population was 83 million with a growth rate of 2.5% against 5.5 million in Ireland. (Indiana 5.8). By 1996 it was still one of the poorest nations but it had greatly improved its position on the world indicator tables. The per capita GNP had risen to 260 UD dollars, life expectancy at birth had increased to 58 years, school enrollment was 58% and the population was 121.6 million with the growth rate reduced to 1.6%. This compares favorably with the Government targets of 1977 although it is always difficult to be certain of the success of population control policies since the developed world rates of population just decreased as the standard of living increased.

We spent 4-weeks in Bangladesh and then returned to Washington DC for about 10-days to write the final report. I was the first to finish so we all retired to the conference room to consider my report: " - on page two you state "-----", what is the basis for that statement ? - it went on for two hours after which I went out fairly drained, assumed my report was terrible and I would never get another mission. Later I learned that was not the case, rather they use the first report to tease out their thoughts on the project.I learned that no experienced consultant finishes a report first. It was like an initiation.

As communications improved, we were able to do our draft reports in the field and final reports at home forforwarding to the Bank.

'Crossed wires' Dhaka Bangladesh   Tea plantation – Sri Lanka

SRI LANKA

When I was asked to join a mission to Sri Lanka in 1992 I went in search
of a stamp album which had survived about fifty years in the attic
because my abiding memory of Ceylon was a picture of tea-plucking on a
tea plantation on an early 20th century postage stamp. I also found a 2
cents stamp with the face of the English King George V and a woman
tapping rubber as well as a more recent 10 cents stamp of King Coconut
and an Adam's peak. I did three supervision missions to Sri Lanka
between 1992 and 1994 in respect of ongoing health and general
education projects.

At that time the social indicators showed Sri Lanka considerably better
off than the other countries of South Asia with 72 years life expectancy
at birth against 53 to 60 years for Bangladesh, India and Pakistan, child
malnutrition at 37% against 40% to 67%, primary school enrollment at
100% against 65% and illiteracy rate of 12% against 52% to 65%.
Although still among the poorer countries of the world, the per capita
GNP was 540 against 220 to 410 USD. Sri Lanka was a little behind the
Philippines economically.

The health project aimed to improve the health and nutrition status of
the people throughout the country and increase the effectiveness of
primary health care including family planning services by upgrading the
physical facilities, equipment and staff as necessary. The education
project consisted mostly of support for upgrading the general education

system including primary and secondary schools, management strengthening and education policy development.

The projects were started so a supervision mission meant office work in the Ministry checking contract documents, procurement procedures and disbursements to ensure compliance with the Staff Appraisal Report. For the architect it also meant a lot of site inspections to see what was being built, to what standard and to ensure that implementation was proceeding to the agreed work program. I was not allowed visit the northern or eastern provinces for security reasons but I got to maybe fifty facilities throughout seven of the nine provinces.

My greatest surprise was to see how different Sri Lanka was to the rest of South Asia. With bell-shaped shrines and dagobas dotting the countryside it was culturally like Thailand. The island, lying between 6 and 10 degrees north of the Equator, is about the size of West Virginia or 75% that of Ireland and has a population of over 18 million. The relief map of the island may generally be said to comprise a mountainous area in the center ranging in elevation between 1,000 to 2,000 meters above sea level, surrounded by an upland area of 300 to 1,000 meters running down to a coastal plain. Ireland is the reverse, it is like a saucer with a central plain and mountains around the coast.

In the third century BC, the king of India sent his friend the King of Ceylon the message of the Buddha and from that time the island embraced Buddhism.

Ceylon's recorded history begins in the 6th century AD, from which time the royal line of 180 Sinhalese kings was maintained for over 2,000 years. Relics of this great dynasty can be seen in the glorious centers of Buddhist architecture, now the ruined cities of Anuradhapura, Polonnaruwa and Sigiriya. Later for over 400 years the island was occupied successively by the Portuguese, Dutch and finally the British, who ruled for over 150 years. Nationalism emerged towards the end of the 19th century but Ceylon gave full support to Britain and the Allies during the Second World War after which the country moved peacefully to independence in 1948.

With the adoption of a new constitution in 1972, the island became a free Sovereign Republic and the name reverted to the original Sri Lanka meaning a Splendid Land. Plantation agriculture was developed by the British and the three major crops; tea, rubber and coconuts, formed the foundation of the economy.

I set off on the first field-trip with Kalum and Kithsiri from the project office going north-east from Colombo through Kurunegala in the coconut area where one can see harvesters climbing the trees at their ease to gather the fruit at the tops. We stopped regularly on all the trips for the cool and refreshing drinks of king-coconut which were obviously very popular and on sale along the roads.

We stayed that night at the Rest House in Polonnaruwa where they put me in room number one, which they proudly announced was the room occupied by the English Princess Elizabeth and her husband during a visit before she became Queen. Early next morning we visited the Gal Vihera Temple to see the colossal stone sculptures of the Buddha in different positions; standing, sitting and particularly the famous reclining statue.

Next morning, my companions asked what I would like to see that day, to which I replied ten facilities, 5 health centers and 5 schools of the project as well as a tea plantation. On the way we stopped to see the amazing 5th century rock palace fortress at Sigiriya and later to see the impressive cave temple at Dambulla although I thought it smelt of bat manure.

In the afternoon near Kandy, we called to a tea plantation where I was initially disappointed because the tea-plucking was only worked in the mornings, avoiding the hottest part of the day but my colleagues arranged a dozen tea pluckers, complete with head scarves and baskets to create the picture of the postage stamp of my youth. Apparently, for the success of the tea industry, they like sun in the morning and some rain in the afternoon.

Reclining Buddah, Gal Vihara, Polonnaruwa

The next field-trip was south along the beautiful coast road as far as the fishing port of Hambantota and on the way we spotted the "toddy-tappers" high in the palm trees, collecting the milky sap from which the popular local alcoholic beverage is made. During that season in Africa, I remember cyclists weaving their way home and it was "the width of the road that bothered them, not the length". We stayed overnight at the lovely old fort town of the present day city of Galle.

Next day we set off to see another 10 facilities and this time a rubber plantation. We traveled inland through Ratnapura with Adams Peak to the left where we stayed overnight in the temperate mountain area of Bandarawela, a fruit and vegetable growing region. Earlier we had stopped to watch men tapping the latex into buckets, which were then taken to the rubber factory where managers seem always ready to welcome visitors. Next day we went on to Badulla before turning down through Nuwara Eliya, the heart of this tea growing country, to Kandy which has been a favorite resort for centuries. It is the center of Sri Lankan culture, nestling in the foothills of the hill-country on the banks of a tree-lined lake beside which stands the Temple of the sacred tooth of the Buddha, which is paraded ceremonially around the city during the most important festival of the year.

It was on a mission to Sri Lanka I discovered I was the only one of four members that did not have a laptop computer so as I sat in the hotel business center, dictating my report to a charming Sinhalese lady, I decided it was time I too got into this new age of communication. Some time a little later I rang Lina Domingo at the Bank to tell her proudly that I had now joined the computer race and was well into word-perfect and lotus but I knew from the delight in her voice that she took great pleasure in welcoming me while adding gleefully that they had just left that software for word and excel so I'd have to start again.

I was on mission in the Philippines in 1993 and had to break off after two weeks to go to Sri Lanka for one week. I flew from Manila to Kuala Lumpur early Saturday and went on from there to Colombo on Sunday afternoon which gave me a little time to get a feeling for KL as I had never been there before. Kuala Lumpur is a curious blend of old and new and I stayed in a modern high-rise development area of offices, hotels and shopping centers. As I went for a walk that evening amidst the buzz of the international architectural construction and traffic, I literally had to dodge some rats, obviously disturbed by the melee, crossing the path in front of me. Modern KL is impressive and it was wonderful to see the economy booming although it was really the old Malaya I had come to see.

Early next morning, I went back into Merdeka Square and walked from the tourist office to the lovely Sultan Abdul Samad building, the oldest landmark of Moorish design, the Secretariat featured on old postage stamps and the heart of colonial KL with the Selangor Club and cricket ground opposite. I continued on to the newer National Mosque built since independence and on to the beautiful arabesque Railway Station. I worked my way by the Jame Mosque in the centre of the new KL and then back to the hotel prior to my departure for Sri Lanka.

Sri Lanka: Building site 1992 and School visit 1994

After finishing in Colombo, I returned to Manila the following week stopping off in Singapore which I have got to know quite well over the years. On one occasion as we drove from Changi airport to the city, it was pointed out to us that the straight dual-carriageway could be turned into an additional flight runway, with the potted trees along the center removed, in forty minutes in an emergency.

Stamford Raffles had changed Singapore from a small fishing village in the early 19th century to a great trading city with a military and naval base but the Second World War changed everything again. If Ireland's departure in 1920 showed the vulnerability of the British Empire in the early 1900s, the fall of Singapore in 1942 was its death knell. It was Britain's Asian bastion which they believed was invincible but fall it did and with such speed, that even the conquering Japanese General was surprised. He had led a swift attack down the Malay peninsula and the defenders were so surprised that he took Singapore with a force that the British outnumbered by three to one. Mary Kenny in her book "Germany Calling" mentioned a rumor of the time never substantiated, that when announcing the fall of Singapore, Lord Haw-Haw declared that the Japanese marched into the city to the strains of an Irish rebel song. The British Commander a Major Perceval had as a young man been sent to

Ireland with the notorious "Black and Tans", an undisciplined despised force sent to put down the Irish rebellion.

Even though Singapore was returned to Britain after the war, it was a changed city and the ruling sentiment was that the only leaders Singaporeans could rely on were their own. It moved towards independence, becoming self-governing in 1959 and after a period 1963-65 when it was part of Malaysia, it finally became an independent city-republic in 1965. The modern Singapore could validly be said to be the creation of Lee Kuan Yew, the first Prime Minister. Although now retired as PM, he is still a major influence throughout South-East Asia. Emerging Nations consulted him on administration and economics and I noted during my time in Vietnam, he was invited there five times to advise the Government.

The best way to see Singapore is to walk but this should be done early morning as the city is almost on the Equator and always hot and humid. I stayed at the west end of the central Orchard Road from which there are good walks to Raffles city, Little India, Arab Street and Chinatown. One of my favorite trips is to take the cable-car from Mount Faber high over the harbor to Sentosa Island, go around the island on the monorail and return by the ferry.

The orchid is the symbol of Singapore so I went to see the orchid garden at the Botanic Gardens, a short walk from the west end of Orchard Road. There one can get an orchid dipped in gold, a great idea and makes a beautiful piece of jewelry. Singapore is still a major crossroads from Europe, Asia and Australia and with its passion for order and cleanliness has become a favorite rest stop from the hectic life of the other cities in the region. People with a little more time usually cross the causeway from the almost antiseptic city state, where jaywalking, spitting, eating chewing gum and failure to flush a public toilet are illegal acts commanding on the spot fines, to the more relaxed traditional Malay Peninsula.

PAKISTAN

Twelve years after my Bangladesh project I found myself on mission in Pakistan, the former West Pakistan before East Pakistan seceded as Bangladesh in 1973.

Poet-philosopher Muhammad Iqbal articulated the concept of Pakistan in its basic form in 1931, when he proposed a separate state comprising the Moslem majority areas in north-western India. The All-India Moslem League led by Muhammad Ali Jinnah adopted the concept in 1940 and the Moslem State that emerged from the partition of British India in 1947 included an eastern wing comprising the eastern half of Bengal province and parts of Assam.

The announcement of the new borders resulted in the greatest migration in human history as some eight million Muslims left India and the same number of Hindus journeyed in the opposite direction. This took place amid terrible bloodshed, suffering, loss and bitterness. Punjab saw the worst as it was divided and the new boundary even cut between the two bigger cities of the Capital Lahore and Amritsar. India got the leading architect Le Corbusier, to design a new Indian Punjap capital at Chandigarh.

Unlike India, Pakistan inherited no well tried machinery of government so that the new country had virtually to start from scratch. Economic survival became the major priority so leaders had to concentrate on internal affairs and political adjustment. Pakistan was proclaimed a strict Moslem Republic in 1956, subject to Sharia law and traditional dress where women wear at least the chador but more often the burka, particularly in the north. A federal parliamentary system was established and continued until Field Marshal Ayub Khan seized power in 1958 and proclaimed a Presidential system in 1962. Civilian government returned from 1970 to 1977 and again in 1988.

Pakistan did well in many ways and by 1990 the per capita GNP was ahead of India and Bangladesh, on a par with Nigeria and about half that of the Philippines, the indicators for child malnutrition were similar but their primary school enrollment and illiteracy rates were way behind with Bangladesh as was the position of women. Although the rights of women are protected by the constitution and women have achieved the highest positions in the land, most lead very traditional lives and their background dictates that they will have little chance of entering the professional fields. Official statistics showed that only 14% have had any schooling and in a survey of 15 of 75 districts, only 1% of women could read or write.

I arrived in Karachi in the early hours of the morning, yet when the doors of the aircraft opened, one was hit by the hot humid air which I felt I could cut with a knife. As the commercial, administrative and educational center of Sindh, it has expanded into a sprawling, bustling metropolis in which since 1947 the population had grown from 400,000 to perhaps 7 million. Karachi was the capital of the country until Islamabad was completed in 1961. On arrival at the Sheraton Hotel, I received a message that the first mission meeting was set for 12 noon. Awaking about 10.30am and drawing back the curtains of the seventh storey window there in the park below men dressed in white were playing cricket, a passion of Pakistanis whose heros were their leading players and throughout our stay we noted pictures of Imran Khan in most public places.

That first evening the mission, perhaps over adventurouslydined at a Japanese restaurant but next day one of the men did not feel at all well after all the raw fish. I learnt that another of the team had once experienced an hotel fire in Manila and although very modest about the experience, played a very courageous part saving others. Since that time he and now I have always carried 50 meters of parachute rope in my luggage on the basis I suppose that like insurance, if you have it you will never need it.

The Indus River is the main artery of the country, rising in the Karakoram mountains in the far north and together with it's tributaries flows through the Punjab and Sindh to a great delta south of Karachi and into the Arabian Sea. Pakistan is a land of hugh contrasts: rich fertile plains by the river basins, arid tracts of the Thar desert, inhospitable barren ranges of Baluchistan and the North West Frontier to the high rugged snow-capped mountains of the Hindu Kush.

The people too are a kaleidoscope of cultures and races all bound together by the Islam, symbolized by the great Shah Faisal Mosque in the Capital and Sharia Law. In the two missions of three weeks each between 1990 and 1993 I visited Islamabad, Peshawar, Karachi and Lahore using each as a base for field-trips to facilities.

The first project was to assist the Government promote family health with new or upgraded facilities at Provincial Headquarters. They included 6 Divisional and 16 District Headquarters in NWF Province Health Centers, Nursing Schools, Basic Health Units and Tehsil Hospitals and similar facilities in Sindh including Taluka Hospitals and Filter Clinics. The second project was in respect of a Population and Family Health program in the Punjab, NWF and Sindh, They included Regional Training Institutes, Provincial Offices and Health Centers, some with accommodation for Surgical Training. Accordingly, the architect again became the "tourist" and in all, I visited about forty facilities in the three provinces.

My field-trips took me through the daily free-for-all in Karachi with the ever pervasive smell of fish around the wharfs and a maze of railway tracks, over the Lyari river to Sher Shah colony and around by Nazimabad. Other trips took me by Quaid-I-Azam, the mausoleum of the founder of the nation, MA Jinnah, and we even had an opportunity to visit the old city with its maze of bazaars.

Beyond Karachi we drove about 180 km to Hyderabad through a barren land until we got near Kotri where we entered the fertile plain of the Indus. We crossed the river to a nurses' college and training institute at Jamshoro and meet the Health Authorities in Hydrabad, one of the oldest cities of the sub-continent.

Buildings in the old city are topped by wind catchers, known as *badgirs* which stand on the rooftops like chimney cowels to catch the breeze which generally come from the one direction during the hottest time of the year. We then traveled on the west side of the river to Thatta, a onetime center for Islamic art and dominated by a great mosque built by the Moghul Emperor Shah Jehan, who was responsible for the Taj Mahal in Agra. Returning to Karachi we passed the Makli Hills, the vast necropolis where the dynasties of Sindh built enormous tombs said to contain one million graves. Many of them are beautifully carved, some glazed and all being restored, making the site a most interesting art gallery.

From Karachi we flew over 1,600 km to Peshawar, Capital of the North West Frontier Province, center of transit trade between the Indian Sub-continent and Persia, Central Asia and the onetime British "Outpost of Empire". We stayed at the Pearl-Continental Hotel which had a small dark lounge-bar hidden in the corner of the foyer with a sign over the door which read "for foreigners and non-Moslem guests only". It is a province of contrasts, mostly rugged and barren but also very fertile where water is available. In places, both temperate and tropical fruit and vegetables grow close together and domestic gardens have hedges of banana plants sheltering patches of carrots and cabbages. Legends abound in British folklore about the NWF and particularly the three great mountain passes - Kyber, Kohat and Malakand. Britain's many attempts to subdue the area were mostly unsuccessfully so that even today the laws of Pakistan do not apply to the Federally Assisted Tribal Areas.Called FATA these are known to belong to the fiercely independent Pathan group of peoples. For security reasons it is not normally advisable for non-Pathans to visit the wild and untamed FATA. Among the sites I visited in Peshawar were the Health Visitors' and Nurses schools, the Regional Training Institute and Lady Reading Teaching Hospital where the main requirements were their necessary upgrading to suit the services proposed and the lack of maintenance over the years.

From Peshawar we made some great trips: one to see the district hospital at Kohat and the tehsil hospital at Hangu which meant driving through the arid desolate Kohat pass in the FATA. We passing through Darra's Bazaar where we were not allowed to stop or take photographs although we could see clearly all the guns in the open stores on both sides of the street. Apparently behind the stores are the workshops where the Zarghuan Khel Afridis produce the most sophisticated weaponry but it is important to stay clear when they start testing the guns by firing indiscriminately.

Another memorable trip took me to Saidu Sharif where I stayed overnight at the Swat Serena Hotel in the beautiful Swat Valley of terraced farming and high snow-capped mountains. In the evening a bus of adventurous tourists arrived before heading next day to Gilgit and the Karakoram highway. They were mostly middle-aged widows and by a strange coincidence one of the ladies had come from my home city. On the way from Peshawar we turned north at Nowshera, noted for its orchards of apples and mangoes on adjoining fields, where I visited another tehsil hospital. We called to the district hospital at Mardan, where there is a major ordnance factory but is noted for its climate where sugar beet and sugar cane are cultivated side by side. At Takht-I-Bahi, there is an old Buddhist temple and then climbed the rugged road along the side of the mountain, through the Malakand Pass before dropping down to the river valley and Saidu.

Next stop was Lahore, capital of the Punjab and cultural center of Pakistan. It has dozens of colleges, schools and all year round displays of art, music and dancing. Lahore Fort gives a good illustration of Moghul history and the famous Shalimar Gardens consisting of terraces, lakes and waterfalls was built at the time of Shah Jahan. The magnificent Badshahi Mosque with its gardens, beautiful marble domes and towering minarets stands out among numerous mosques and shrines. Lahore is a good place to see the ordinary life of the country with painted trucks, bullock carts, handcarts, cars, buses and scooters. A whole family can ride a scooter with mother riding side-saddle holding the baby and the toddler standing in front of the driver, holding on to the handlebars.

We stayed at the Avari Hotel and by another coincidence I had dinner there one evening with Colm MacGiolla Ri, one of my golfing partners from home who was there. He was on an itinerant consultancy in respect of transport.

Lahore is well served with health facilities and we visited the UCH, Fatima Memorial, Lady Willington and Ganga Ram Hospitals as well as some regional and non-clinical training Institutes as well as the District Hospital 70 kilometers north in a fertile farmland area at Gugranwala famous for it's fruit.

Finally we returned to Islamabad, the new capital since 1961, to prepare our reports for the wrap-up meetings with the Government. Islamabad is a twin city of Rawalpindi but while the latter, the headquarters for the army, is an old traditional city with crowded streets, narrow winding bazaars and old buildings, the new city is spaciously laid out on a grid with plenty of trees and landscaping beneath the Margalla Hills. A stranger once asked "where is Islamabad" to which he got the reply "15 km from Pakistan".

Situated on the border of the Punjab and NWF Provinces, the seismic zoning map shows it to be an area liable to moderate damage and it was here that I experienced my first earthquake. After lunch one day I was doing something with my case when suddenly I felt a strange sensation, the lid of the case closed and turning, I noticed the standard lamp was swaying. It was over in 2 or 3 seconds and I stepped out into the corridor just as my neighbour was also coming out. We just looked at one another and he said "yes, it was a little earthquake". I visited the hospitals in Islamabad and Rawalpindi which were to have additional maternity and child health facilities as well as some other services. The construction industry was not well organised and the process was considered to be inefficient and slow but I was encouraged during my field-trips because although the general standard of finish was not high there was an absence of serious structural defects in spite of the fact that there was little maintenance carried out for many years.

AFRICA

RETURN TO NIGERIA

I arrived back in Lagos airport in January 1984, 19 years after my earlier departure and some 10 days after the army had again seized power. After touchdown the pilot announced that we should remain calmly in our seats as army personnel would pass through the airplane. When the doors opened soldiers marched down the passages, guns at the ready, tensely scrutinizing everybody and watchful for any possible opposition to the recent coup. It was a most uncomfortable experience.
In 1861 the small kingdom of Lagos was ceded to Britain by its ruler Dosonmu and this was the first time they occupied land in what is now the Federation of Nigeria. One hundred years later, Lagos became the Capital of the largest independent nation of Africa.
I had been appointed as a freelance consultant, under the United Nations Development Program to advise on the preparatory assistance required in respect of the draft project document, for the development of Abuja

and impact area of the new Capital, by focusing on the shelter needs of the lowest income groups.

The changes in Nigeria since our departure in 1965 were staggering. Lagos's population had grown to perhaps 10 million making it one of the the most congested cities in Africa, full of people, vehicles and buildings from hovels to skyscrapers.

Lagos grew from a settlement of the 15th century, which developed as a trading post which in turn presaged the foreign colonizing of the interior. Lagos spread across a number of islands, linked to the mainland by one bridge. Because of the poor bearing capacity of the ground, there were few buildings above 3-storeys in height by the 1960s. The oil boom of the 1970s changed the infrastructure and face of Lagos beyond recognition and the use of pile foundations and more reliable lifts enabled the construction of high-rise buildings while air-conditioning, which was becoming common, facilitated deep compact planning. The new and expanded docks of Tin Can Island and Apapa, the new Murtala Muhammad airport at Ikeja and the expansion of the city were now linked by ring roads and major highways.

Lagos is divided into a number of distinct areas based on its island nature and it had been necessary to reclaim swamp land before the city could develop. Previously Lagos Island was the heart of the city with most of the commercial and administrative headquarters, large shops and offices while Ikoyi island was the major residential area with beautifully landscaped houses, gardens and clubs. Victoria Island was undeveloped, the port was at Apapa, industry and further residential expansion occurred on the mainland, across Carter Bridge. By the 1980s all the swamps of the Metropolitan area, including large areas of Victoria, Ikoyi and Apapa islands, were reclaimed and linked by elevated road - ways, some up to 100 meters out over what had previously been sea. On this occasion, my trip only lasted a few days due to the political uncertainty at that time. I was to visit one of the Ministries in the new

Capital of Abuja but, just as I was due to travel, the Development Authority Offices were taken over by the National Security Officers and Army Intelligence to carry out an investigation into allegations of corruption. The offices were expected to be closed for about ten days so rather than wait in Lagos, the mission was abandoned and I went home to await a better time.

General Buhari had turned out to be a rigid and uncompromising leader, censoring the press and detaining the opposition without trial. He was replaced in an August 1985 palace-coup by General Babangida who instituted constitutional reform and undertook to return the country to civilian government.

I had just returned again, a week earlier, as part of a World Bank team on mission to review the strategy and content of a primary health care project. My brief related to the construction, and management activities undertaken under the project. I was to travel to Sokoto State in the far northwest sub-tropical savanna, the Moslem capital and seat of the Sultan.

On the way, I visited Kaduna and it was most interesting to see all the changes over the previous 20 years. The population had grown by over a million people and the infrastructure had expanded greatly but much of the Kaduna I had known was still recognisable. I toured the city and surrounding areas we had known, visited the houses in which Dympna and I had lived and it was amazing to see the planting of the 1950s and 1960s now grown to full maturity. A missionary friend suggested that planting was not often vandalized. *He suggested that trees were much safer than people.*

Although the city had retained much of its previous character, it was sadly showing a lack of maintenance since the political deterioration and economic downturn. The parks and open spaces were no longer maintained and Kaduna had acquired the violence of the larger cities with religious strife regularly between Moslem and Christian in which many were killed.

I went on to Sokoto by car and was joined on the mission by Richard Brown a wonderfully entertaining US American Public Health Specialist who arrived from a Baptist missionary hospital near Kinshasa in Zaire. He had a passion for Kipling and insisted on counting my beers in the evening.

Large expatriate construction companies often set up club facilities for their employees and we had heard that there was one not far from the Sokoto Hotel. One Sunday morning we set off to find this club, hoping for a change of lunch menu. We found it without difficulty but as their construction works were nearing completion, few people were around and the restaurant was closed.

A Swede sitting by the pool asked us if we knew about the coup which had taken place in Lagos that morning. He informed us that a dusk to dawn curfew had been declared for all the State Capitals. We hadn't heard so we returned to the hotel without delay and discussed what we would do if the situation became serious.

I suggested that as he was an US citizen and we were on a World Bank mission, the US would probably send an helicopter to take us to their embassy in Lagos. This did not appeal to him so he suggested we should go north and when we got to an east-west asphalt road, not far away, we would be in the Niger Republic and could make our way to Niamey. However, that evening traffic seemed the same as usual and the curfew did not materialize in Sokoto State.

We were collected next morning to go to the Ministry of Health about an hour later than usual and on our arrival we noted groups of men obviously discussing the political events. Later in the day, however, when it was established that the new administration had only been an internal palace coup and the influence of the North was not diminished, life settled back to normal quickly and we finished our mission successfully. A project colleague in the World Bank headquarters, David Radel, had very kindly telephoned my wife to advise her of the situation only to find that Dympna had already received a similar communication of

reassurance from the Embassy of Ireland in Lagos, through the
Department of Foreign Affairs in Dublin.

On completion of our work, I departed by road to the airport in Kano, the
largest of the ancient Hausa cities and a major terminus of trans-
Saharan trade for many centuries. There is a wonderful view of the old
Tudan Wada from the minarets of the Kano Central Mosque, designed
and built by the Ministry of Works in 1948. There too one meets the
"Blue Men" of the desert in their dark blue regas and turbans who have
long captured the worlds' imagination through their mastery of one of
the most inhospitable regions and their fierce independence. The
Tuaregs, a light skinned Berber
people are famous for their camel caravans and nomadic border-less
lives in the no-man's-land between Black Africa below the Sahara and
Arab Africa above it.

Dye-works, Zaria NigeriaBoat-shop on Halong Bay, Vietnam

I went back to Nigeria again in 1985, as part of another World Bank
mission, for the preparation of a health project in Imo State, in the
Southeast tropical forest area,. The people of Imo, mainly Ibo or Igbo,
are Christian as a result of many close relationships they formed with
Irish Missionaries. They are bright and well educated, talented and
industrious and as a consequence are probably impatient for
development and intolerant of others less capable than themselves.
The Ibos like to enjoy themselves and on one occasion in 1986, we
attended the annual yam festival at Mbano, presided over by the Eze or
village chief. There, our mission leader Stan Scheyer was asked to select

the best yam of the day and although he had no expertise in yams, he obviously made a good choice with the help of the mission members and we were made to very welcome.

Each woman wore a bupa or dress complete with a gele draped in an exotic turban style of a particular color depending on her circumstance, blue for those married and living in the village, yellow for married women originally from the village but now living elsewhere and a third color for single women, making the whole festival very colorful and musical as dancing occupies a unique place in Ibo life. Music is the principal medium through which they express the whole range of their experience and emotions.

Tuaregs, the "Blue Men" of the desert

I was to return on Bank Supervision missions to the Sokoto and Imo Projects regularly from 1985 to 1990 and had the wonderful opportunity of getting to know those contrasting States extensively. At that time the Government was implementing a Structural Adjustment Program at the insistence of the International Monetary Fund and I remember thinking, there must be an easier way. On one occasion during the implementation of the program, I was considering the purchase of one of three paintings, they were 30 naira each and the naira was artificially kept on parity with the USD in order to keep prices down for the people. However, as part of the structural adjustment, the Government floated the currency one Thursday afternoon and the naira fell immediately to a rate of five to the USD. I bought all three pictures for 90 naira, now a total of 18 USD against the 90 USD that morning. The cost of living began to escalate and during the next mission, people showed me the small bowl of cassava they got for their naira whereas some months earlier they got five such bowls for the naira. Life became extremely difficult for the people and this was reflected in all the economic and social indicators. Similarly, with regard to the Globalisation policies being promoted towards the end of the century, should the poorer States be asked to trade on an equal basis with the richer ones? Surely the United Nations or World Trade Organisation chould come up with a fairer system as in the game of golf where weaker players are given an handicap so they can compete more equally with the best.

The Preparation and Supervision Teams in Imo State, Nigeria

Sometimes the Ministry of Health involved in the project would host a dinner for the mission and on one occasion the man beside me, a Secretary of Department, learning I was from Ireland inevitably asked about the troubles in the North. I gave him my views as a Nationalist and he said that one of my Bishops had said the opposite and when I looked perplexed he confirmed what aChurch of Ireland Bishop had said. What could I say but try to explain that the "Church of Ireland" was not really what it seemed but rather a colonial anomaly similar if for example they made the Anglican Church Missionary Society the established Church of Nigeria.

On a similar occasion in another State a Department Secretary in conversation expressed the view that he could not understand why Ireland wanted independence from Britain or indeed why the Crown allowed it. Both seemed incomprehensible to him and it was interesting for me to learn how some others see us.

I was a "one man" mission for a couple of subsequent visits because at the last moment the supervision of other components would be postponed. I learned some time afterwards that a major reason for my one-man missions was that it was difficult to get people willing to travel to Nigeria because of the reputation it had acquired. Murtala Muhammad airport, Ikeja had become a dreadful experience so I had refined my baggage to carry-on units only, to avoid the baggage recovery hall. There one never knew if the baggage would arrive in one piece and if it did one may have to "buy" it back from the handlers. Immigration too was formidable; the passport was delivered through a small hole in a central cubicle glazed with a dark one-way mirror so that one could not see inside. One waited indefinitely perspiring anxiously in a milling crowd until hopefully one heard the passport number called and subsequently it appeared through another hole.

Later at a mission dinner, a senior government official expressed the hope that Nigeria might soon develop a tourist industry and I could only try to visualise a 'blue-rinse brigade' arriving from the US and within 10 minutes returning in a panic to the airplane to depart again as soon as possible.

Baggage halls seem to be the low-point of air-travel. I arrived once at JFK New York from Nigeria to note my bag on the carousel had a broken strap and the lid zip half open. I went straight to a customs officer to inform him of my problem and ask him to accompany me to the carousel to witness my opening of the bag in case something may have been added. He did not want to know and told me to take the bag away to some quiet area to open it. My camera and sandals had been removed and I was waved through customs without question. I wonder if his attitude would be different two decades later after September 11-2001. The supervision of the civil works sub-component of the service delivery was a distinct element so a one-man mission could go ahead independently. The architect was sometimes considered the "tourist" of the team, since he was required to travel extensively and see as many of the facilities in the project as possible.

Some of the district hospitals were not administered to an adequate standard so on one occasion I suggested we visit a comparable catholic mission hospital run by nuns. There the standard was impeccable, clean and orderly with the staff rota for the year on the notice board in the matron's office and the compound landscaped and maintained. The doctor from the Ministry, who accompanied us, took me aside later to say he thought the idea was great as he had been trying to convey the same message. He added that during the Biafran war he had been stationed at that same hospital to attend the wounded.

During another double-mission to both Imo and Sokoto States, I was joined in Owerri by Lina Domingo, a colleague from Washington DC, who did not care to travel alone in Nigeria so I took a car down the 80 km to meet her on arrival at the airport in Port Harcourt. On my way to the airport, we were stopped by bandits who had stretched a large pole across the road to block passage. Luckily, the driver spoke the same language, established friendly contact with two of the bandits and after an anxious fifteen minutes, we were allowed pass. During the negotiations, I pretended to be busily writing in my notebook. Further along, the road forked and two policemen stepped out with hands raised to halt us but the driver swerved to avoid them and carried on. Tongue-in-cheek, I asked him what happened back there and with a smile he told me it was not wise to stop for Nigerian policemen.

For Sokoto missions I usually flew into Kano Airport where in earlier years visitors were greeted by a colorful Hausa-man riding a camel and playing the long traditional horn of welcome.I was met there on one occasion by the Project Manager John Dubey.

Groundnut pyramid Kano 1960s   *Kano Mosque built in 1948*

John was a most interesting if enigmatic American convert to Islam. He had previously worked for many years in the adjoining francophone areas of Africa and was now very "at home" in Africa. He also seemed to have a detailed knowledge of the highways and byways of Ireland and I seem to remember that his father was Arab, mother French and nanny Irish but I may be wrong. During one mission, he proudly showed me his newly born Nigerian son. Over the years, it seemed a characteristic of international operatives, a colourful array of very interesting if sometimes complex, unorthodox and independently minded personalities.

ABUJA - THE NEW CAPITAL

At the end of one large project review mission in Sokoto, I traveled south with a Zairian Public Health Specialist across the country to Owerri, capital of Imo State. On the way we stopped in the old mud-walled city of Zaria to see the distinctive architecture of decorated earthen houses. Earthen construction is used extensively throughout the world and accounts for some 50% of rural and 20% of urban building in the developing world. Its characteristic appearance leaves an indelible stamp on the architecture between the 30 degree lines of latitude north and south. It is used not only for housing but also for public buildings across the Sahel, North Africa and the Middle East and throughout all tropical-dry areas. The Palaces of the Fulani/Hausa Emirs of Nigeria and the Mosques of Mali are particularly good examples.

The use of unbaked earthen construction has many advantages both economically, environmentally and socially. The material is local so avoids the importation of expensive alternatives.It does not contribute to the deforestation resulting from the necessity of firing or processing other materials and much of the excavated material arising from large public works such as roads can be recycled. It therefore avoids the pollution which can otherwise arise.

The traditional methods of construction employed mean that buildings can be implemented by the communities themselves and harmonise with the landscape and the culture of the people. Building maintenance thenbecomes part of the normal rhythm of community life.

We also drove through the onetime capital Kaduna and later after passing the large rock-mountain, the Zuma inselberg, rising abruptly from the level landscape we arrived at the new Federal Capital Territory of Abuja. There we stayed overnight in the luxury of the recently completed Nicon Noga Hilton Hotel, not far from the Presidential complex.

Emir's Palace, Zaria, 1961

Lagos, the previous capital, had been bursting at the seams as it had continued to act as the Federal, State and Commercial Capital as well as the major port of the country, so a distinguished panel was appointed to consider the adequacy of this triple role. The Aguda Panel reported to the Government in 1975 that for many reasons, including the inadequacy of suitable land, Lagos was considered unsuitable to continue in its present roles.

Kaduna had become identified with the oligarchy of the North during the first decades of independence, so the Military Government decided in 1976 that Nigeria should have a new Federal Capital near the old town of Suleija and the complete transfer of the Capital was scheduled for 1986. In the new Abuja plan, the road from the airport leads in a double axis to the city center. The city is laid out on a square grid leading, by the executive buildings, to a circular climax focusing on the National Assembly with Presidential complex and Supreme Court to either side. The residential districts, parallel to the main axis, were planned in a freer form within curved avenues and roads, off which public buildings and facilities form local features. The overall plan is fan-shaped and like Brasilia and Chandigarh, the roads are the means by which the plan is identified so the city is defined by expressways and ring roads.

From Abuja we crossed the Niger River above Lokoja, where the Benue River joins the Niger and we continued south, deep into the tropical forest. We crossed the Niger again at Onitsha, where Dympna and I had crossed by ferry for the first time in 1961 before the bridge was built. The river is a few kilometers wide at this point but had been perhaps a few hundred meters wider before the necessary filling done as part of the construction of the new bridge. We continued south in the heart of the industrious Ibo country to Owerri, capital of Imo State. In the center of the city there is a large and impressive Cathedral, built by Bishop Joseph Whelan with shamrocks and harps worked into the stained glass windows and the artwork showed his Irish background.

During the 2-day trip my Zairean companion told me the following fascinating personal story: His mother was very young when given in marriage to his father. She conceived a few times but sadly all were lost before birth. Her uncle took her to his home, to look after her until she was more mature and when he decided she was ready, he brought her back to her husband. In a short time she again conceived and subsequently gave birth to a healthy baby boy. She, her husband and all their friends and family were ecstatic with joy, "miatadila", "wonderful" they cried. Because of their special delight they decided to call the boy, "Miatadila". They also thought they should add the uncle's name because he had been so supportive. In many African societies, children were not necessarily given their father's or family name and it is only later in life, when they require a passport or such that they become aware of a first name and surname. Some weeks later when "Miat" was brought to the church to be baptised the priest said the child should have a proper Christian name so he baptised the boy Patrick. Subsequently the boy was always called Miat but whenever he heard his mother call "Pat-rick", he knew he was in trouble.

In 1974 President Mabuto ordered all Zairians with Christian names to drop them in favor of African ones and warned that any priest found baptising a Zairian child with an European name would face a five year jail sentence. The example highlighted the importance of the later canonization of African saints like the Uganda martyrs in 1993 giving the people of Africa, their own Christian names.

Although Imo was a small State densely populated in the tropical forest area with rich vegetation, the roads, which had been damaged during the civil war and not maintained, were in bad condition so travel was long and difficult. I remember Lina and I stopping by the roadside to buy bananas and peanuts for instant energy. However I did manage to see many facilities in towns with typically southern Nigerian names with an Ibo sound like - Owerri, Okigwi, Okposi, and Umuahia - which has it's origins in the languages of Central Africa. During one of the field trips I met and had a meal in the house of one of the army leaders of the Biafran rebellion, where pictures of the war as well as his awards were displayed around the walls. In spite of the dreadful experiences and suffering during that war, I have always been very impressed at the degree of reconciliation that took place afterwards.

For one mission in 1990 during which I expected to be traveling a lot throughout the large Sokoto State, including relatively isolated places, I set-off from home with plastic containers of cereal, coffee, sugar, butter, all the basics and also some goodies available on the outward flight. Thus armed, I arrived at Kano to be met by the Project Construction Manager Yusufu Goronyo who was to accompany me and we stayed the first night in an hotel in Gusau. From there we set off northwards through the dry open countryside inspecting health clinics in villages with such exotic hausa names like Kaura Namoda, Talata Mafara and Birnin Kebbi. Hausa comes from the same language group as Berber and Arabic and sounds very different to that spoken in southern Nigeria. We visited a total of forty clinics in five days, driving for eight hours each day in a 4-wheel-drive vehicle as we bumped across laterite roads and dry riverbeds. My companion Mallam Yusufu, the son of an Imam, was good company for the fieldtrips and we both enjoyed the experience very much. He described his life farming before he went to study construction at the Sokoto College. His religious way of life was very important to him but he was firmly against the fundamental Islamic movement. During one long trip I heard the gentle clacking of his worry-beads as I had my rosary. I became strangely aware that while we were praying side by side we could not pray together. We had discussions on the similarities between Christianity and Islam and agreed there was no valid reason for the hostility or suspicion sometimes voiced between them.

As well as Gusau, we stayed at hotels in Sokoto and Argungu, famous for its spectacular annual fishing festival on the Kebbi river, a tributary of the Niger. All 3-hotels were identical prefabricated 100-bed units which had been brought in from Japan by a Japanese company working in the State. On arrival in Sokoto one evening, Yusufu went home to his family while I booked into the hotel. After a shower and change, I made for the very large dimly lit dining room. Nobody was around so I called out and a steward appeared through the kitchen door at the far end. I asked the position about dinner to be told that I was the only guest and they had no food. He kindly offered to go to the market but I asked only for boiling water and bread, I was glad of my plastic containers so I dined very adequately with the provisions I had carried from home.

It may seem a strange place for it to happen but one of my special memories of Sokoto, the home of the Moslem Sultan, was a Sunday Mass I attended there in a large open covered hall with a congregation of about two thousand. The choir of about one hundred and fifty women, in their best "Sunday clothes" and accompanied by a number of traditional drummers, sang the Mass in the African high-life style as they swayed to the beat giving their colourful and lively interpretation of the liturgy. It was original, authentic and a real celebration.

At the end of the mission, I went by car to Lagos to report to the Bank on project progress. We passed through Yelwa and Bin Yauri where in 1964 I had attended an Emir's council meeting, called to consider the plans for the redevelopment of the town arising from the construction of the Kainji Dam. Much of the existing town would be submerged by the new reservoir and my duty was to advise on the planning and design of some of the new buildings including the Emir's palace.

It was prudent when traveling in Nigeria, to stop by about 4.00pm in the afternoon and certainly before dark. I stayed in the Kwara Hotel in Ilorin where twenty five years earlier, I had designed the house for the new Bishop and in which Cardinal Montini, later Pope Paul VI, stayed during a 1960s visit to Nigeria. Indeed, we ourselves stayed in the house shortly after the Cardinal's departure and enjoyed the goodies remaining. Ilorin had grown enormously since that time and now had a very large and impressive central mosque, one of the largest in the country.

Emir of Yauri Council Meeting 1964   *Mission team, Kano 1992*

The Bank personnel had come to Lagos to review their program in the country and on the Sunday morning as they flew out of Nigeria, I greatly regretted having to set off across the country to Imo State for another week. It was about an 8-hour drive to Owerri with a good highway through the rainforest to Benin City about halfway. I have never liked that city as it always seemed mysterious and forbidding to me but maybe that is because I got caught-up in a demonstration there when passing through it once. It was not pleasant sitting in a car surrounded by a noisy, exited and unpredictable crowd. The countryside after Benin to the River Niger is more open beyond which one enters the land of the mainly Ibo peoples.

My last World Bank mission to Nigeria in 1992 started in Lagos. We were there to help prepare a Secondary Health Care Project, the purpose of which was to revitalise the secondary level of referral or cottage hospitals throughout Nigeria. The mission visited about thirty facilities in seven States in the North, West and East and it was particularly interesting for me since it meant revisiting some of the hospitals we had implemented in the 1960s. The mission found that in general, the earlier buildings were to a higher standard than those carried out post mid-1970s but all had deteriorated due to lack of maintenance for many years. The fieldtrip itself was a wonderful nostalgic experience but for those with us who were not familiar with Nigeria, it gave an exceptional insight to the diversity of geography, peoples and cultures of the country.

We visited hospitals in Ondo State in the West from Okitipupa, in the mangrove swamp area near the coast, to Ado-Ekiti in Abia State in the East. We went to the old eastern capital of Enugu and traveled Anambra State from Abakaliki to Onitsha on the Niger River. There I called to the Cathedral to see the grave of the famous Bishop Joseph Shanahan who had arrived as a missionary in 1902, now resting beside that of his successor Archbishop Charles Heerey. After his death Bishop Shanahan was acclaimed as the father of the great Irish Missionary Movement that marked the first half of the 20th century. He had died in Kenya in 1943 but at public request he was reinterred in 1956 amid great rejoicing in Nigeria where he had spent some 30 of his most successful years.

Government College Katsina, opened in 1922

We visited facilities in Niger State in the center of the country from Minna to Suleija and then flew to Borno State in the far north-east. There we continued facility inspections from Maiduguri to Mongono close to Lake Chad, now much smaller than it in the 1960s due to regular droughts. We went on to Kano State for inspections from Dawaki Kudu to Bichii and stayed at a building company's Impresit Guest House because some years earlier, Dave Radel and I had stayed at the Central Hotel and were woken repeatedly during the night by moneychangers and prostitutes.

We then went on to Katsina State, where I had the great pleasure of visiting one of the cottage hospitals we had designed and built in the 1960s in the semi-desert conditions of Daura on the border with the

Niger Republic. Katsina was the inheritor of the 'Timbuktu tradition' of learning in the Western Sudan. It was a great Saharan market city, famous for their Sallah festivals which are wonderful spectacles with charges of salutation on camel and horseback by the Emir's colorful guards or Dongari. We had attended such a Durbar in Zaria in 1960 in front of the Emir's Palace, where there are exceptional examples of earthen architecture with lavish colored and "embossed" art of mural decoration. In Katsina too the famous Government school in which many of the earlier leaders were educated is now a museum and is a beautifully proportioned example of the earthen architecture of the Sahel. Indeed we do not always realise that a great part of the world bears an indelible stamp of earthen architecture of which the Mosques of Mopti and Djenne in Mali are outstanding examples.

Grand Mosques in Mopti and Djenna, Mali, West Africa

At the end of the 1992 mission to Nigeria, I departed Murtala Muhammad International airport, Lagos for London where I arrived about 5.00am. Dympna had come from home the previous evening with air-tickets and some items for me so I went up to her room in the airport hotel. We had breakfast together and after perhaps a total of 5-hours in London I flew off for Hong Kong en-route to the Philippines. Dympna said I was so excited it seemed "I went with wings on my heels".

MALAWI

I had been to Nigeria twice yearly from 1984 to 1992 so it was wonderful to receive a telephone call in 1993 from the United Nations Educational Scientific and Cultural Organization UNESCO in Paris inviting me to join their Preparation Mission for an Education Project in Malawi. I had never been to Central Africa but had read so much about it because of problems arising from forced evictions to accommodate planters and settlers.

What is now Malawi was settled from the 14th to the 18th centuries by the Bantu. David Livingstone, missionary and explorer, following earlier journeys into Southern Africa, explored the Shire region around the present Blantyre in 1862, discovered Lake Nyasa, "broad water" and laid the foundations for what became Nyasaland.

During this time he encountered the notorious Arab slave trader, Tippoo Tib. It was due to Livingstone's accounts, sent home, that opened the eyes of the world to the horrors of the slave trade and was instrumental in it's abolition. The objective of his later trip was to discover the source of the Nile so he wandered across large tracts from Lake Nyasa to Lake Tanganyika and opened up the whole of Central Africa to the influences of Christianity. He also carried out invaluable mapping and other exploratory work. He was not heard from for about 5 years until that famous encounter at Ujiji in Tanzania with the US American Henry Stanley who had been sent out by the New York Herald to find him or ascertain if he was still alive. Livingstone found it difficult to get financing in Britain for his expeditions but did invaluable work so that when he died near Lake Tanganyika, he was thought of so highly that his followers carried his body across the country to Zanzibar for shipment home. Livingstonia in Northern Malawi was called after him and the commercial city of Blantyre was named after his birthplace.

Cecil Rhodes, who followed, was an adventurer and imperialist whose efforts were directed towards the extension of British rule and the carving up of Africa for British gain. He wanted a British Africa all the way from the Cape to Egypt. In terms of settlement and development Rhodes urged British intervention in Nyasaland so they established it as a British Protectorate in 1891.

Later, planted with settlers although not as extensively as in the neighboring countries where they still present ongoing problems, it became a colony in 1907 when more land was expropriated. Traditional farming was discouraged and a hut tax was introduced so that people had to work in the plantations to survive. The pattern was similar to that applied in Ireland in the 19th century. In 1953 Nyasaland was joined with the Federation of Northern and Southern Rhodesia to form the Central African Federation against the wishes of the people. Opposition then grew against colonialism as a whole, leading to independence in 1964. Malawi was declared a Republic in 1966 and Dr. Hastings Banda, its founder and leader became its first President.

Lying between 9 and 18 degrees south of the equator, it is essentially a small but very beautiful, tranquil and imaginative country. An example of this is the currency called the Kwache and the Tambala, Kwacha means "dawn" and Tambala means "cockerel" and 100 cockerels make a dawn. The main attraction is Lake Nyasa/Malawi, which has an abundance of fish and stretches over 500 km north to south forming it's eastern boundary. The people are very friendly. Music and dance, which has been handed down through the generations, plays an important part in most of their celebrations including puberty, initiations, marriage and death. Unfortunately it seemed Dr. Banda stayed in power too long and became dictatorial and repressive. In 1992 his position became untenable when a group of Catholic bishops called for change and condemned the regime. Donor countries too cut non-humanitarian aid. With his departure, multinational agencies returned and in 1996 government reforms including an International Monetary Fund recommended Structural

Adjustment Program were implemented. With subsidies removed, food prices and unemployment increased leading to great hardship so crime increased as life got harder.

Sadly, Malawi was one of the poorest countries in the world and World Bank indicators showed that while the population increased from 9 to 10 million between 1992 and 1996, the per capita GNP went down from 210 to 180 USD as did life expectancy at birth from 44 to 43 years. However, school enrollment was increasing rapidly from only 54% in 1990 and the overall objective of the project we were to prepare, was to increase opportunities in formal primary and secondary education as well as the improvement of its quality.

Overcrowding in primary schools in the urban areas was a serious problem. The rising population and the drift to the cities over a number of years had increased the average number of children per primary class to nearly 200 pupils. This overcrowding was partly solved by introducing a double-shift system thereby reducing the rate to nearly 100 pupils and physical expansion of the facilities became then the most obvious additional complement. Lack of maintenance of buildings over the years meant that existing schools had become so dilapidated that physical rehabilitation was also essential.

The primary curriculum was eight years, school sizes varied from 8 to 16 classrooms and the particular project objective was to reduce the pupil/class ratio. Since there was already a surplus of teaching staff available, the solution, decided by the mission and government, was to identify a number of towns as a pilot project area, increase the size of all the schools to 16 classrooms each and re-arrange the teaching timetable so that all the schools could operate classes in both double shifts and double streams. The number of pupils per class would thereby be reduced to about 40. The project would be evaluated after a few years and if then considered successful, the concept would be extended to other towns.

To identify the pilot area, it was necessary to inspect the school facilities at selected centres and in this context the capitals of the three regions were chosen: Mzuzu in the north, the Capital Lilongwe in the center and Blantyre in the south so the architect again became the "tourist" of the mission.

We were staying at the Capital Hotel in Lilongwe and my first field-trip took us through typical fertile undulating tropical countryside to Mzuzu some 260 km north. A pleasant provincial town on the Lunyangwa river, we stayed at the Mzuzu Hotel nestled among colourful bougainvillea. We met the education authorities and visited about six representative schools of the seventeen including one under construction to see building standards, as well as three government aided mission schools. We visited the lovely fishing village of Nkhata Bay and returned to Lilongwe by the lakeside road to Salima. The road was mostly of laterite but driving along the coast we passed many tourist rest-houses and beaches including Chintheche and the large town near the entrance to the Nkhotakota National Park.

Our next field-trip was to Blantyre, the commercial and industrial centre set in the hilly country of the Shire Highlands about 310 km south of Lilongwe. On the way for some 30 km south of Dedza, the road is virtually the border between Malawi and Mozambique and it was sad to see all the houses on the latter side roofless and burnt with new housing on the Malawi side where the people had simply crossed the road because of the civil war in Mozambique.

Ryall's Hotel where we stayed was the first hotel built in what was then Nyasaland and had beautifully laid out mature gardens. There we met the education authorities and visited about four primary and two secondary schools including a mission school and one nearing completion. We also went on about 50 km further south to Chikwawa to see a new district office which was under construction. All the construction work seen was very competently carried-out and confirmed that when prudently implemented and supervised, the construction industry in Malawi was reasonably well organised.

Back in Lilongwe, we visited a number of schools including six primary and one of four large secondary schools.

Zomba was the capital until 1975 when Lilongwe, previously a small dusty town on the Lilongwe River, was proclaimed the new capital and is known as a "garden city". It really has two centres, the new Capital Hill of government and administrative offices in modern architecture and landscaped gardens. The old town is much more interesting because of it's traditional African atmosphere. The Capital Hotel where we stayed in a landscaped parkland of tall indigenous trees, exotic jacaranda and hibiscus had a large chess board, with one meter high pieces, laid out on the swimming poolterrace. We enjoyed a couple of games of chess and like all sensible consultants I did not beat the mission leader, a wonderful Dutch gentleman Pierre Baesjau.

After agreeing and assigning responsibility with our government counterparts for the next steps to be undertaken, we departed for UNESCO Paris to complete the preparation report. This was a real bonus because Paris remains our favourite city and Dympna happily joined me there for the week. Part of my work included the preparation of the cost-tables for the project, including all the components, not just civil works. Following my Sri Lanka mission, I had become moderately computer literate but I was intimidated at the thought of half a dozen pages of continuous spreadsheet calculations, with every other column depending on what seemed complicated multiples of others, so I decided to do the whole lot manually. This meant a few very long days and late nights. In the end I was glad I did because I really got to understand the system, which was new to me. When we finished and I got home, I used those tables to learn how to apply the relevant software which I have since used. Shortly it became hard to imagine a world without laptops and email although only a decade in use.

Five months later in 1993 I was again invited by UNESCO Paris to join a Supervision mission to Mozambique. This was my first time working in acommunistcountry with a command economy and it was also immediately post conflict. What I learned there was very helpful when working subsequently in similar countries. Miarro II, a tall gentle man from the Republic of Chad, was the mission leader for the African Development Bank. It was a pleasure to work with him and met him again about five years later in Washington DC after he had retired to do similar consultancies for the World Bank.

MOZAMBIQUE

Mozambique had been a Province of Portugal since the 1890s but dissatisfaction grew after the 1960 Mueda massacre in which government troops opened fire on demonstrators, killing a large number. FRELIMO was formed in 1962 and the war of liberation followed until 1975 when the Peoples' Republic of Mozambique was declared with Samora Machel as President. Portugal withdrew everything immediately, even light bulbs, leaving Mozambique in chaos. Ties were established with the USSR but by 1983 the country was almost bankrupt. South Africa and Rhodesia helped to form the opposition RENAMO and moved to destabilise the government. Drought and famine followed, the socialist experiment had failed and FRELIMO turned to the West in 1984. President Machel was killed in an airplane crash in 1986. His widow subsequently became Nelson Mandela's second wife.

Early 1990 saw Marxist ideology disavowed and protracted negotiations got under way in Rome which led to a peace agreement in October 1992 bringing the long civil-war to an end. The UN monitored the cease-fire and the demobilisation campaign.
It was at this stage that we arrived on mission in November 1993. Mozambique has a 2,000 km coastline of mangroves and marsh vegetation common to coastal estuaries and the Zambesi river delta faces Madagascar in the Indian Ocean.

Tourism from the RSA and Central Africa had been popular with its images of beautiful beaches, waving palm trees, calm lagoons and an abundance of sea-food cooked in piri-piri. It had been a significant source of foreign exchange before independence. That had disappeared and the country was just starting to recover. We failed to get accommodation at a small more African hotel and were staying at the Polana Hotel, known as the "grand old lady" of Africa. It certainly was the best hotel I have seen on the Continent and had just been rehabilitated and upgraded. One guest told me, he saw it three years earlier when it had been a casualty of the war and rats were running down the corridors. Now it was back to it's full grandeur with large swimming pool set in beautiful gardens, additional modern bedrooms in terraces down the steep hill and overlooking the blue Indian Ocean. The tourist advance of uninhibited yuppies from South Africa and Zimbabwe were again starting to arrive.

The World Bank indicators, however, showed Mozambique among the poorest countries with per capita GNP at USD 60 in 1992, having fallen from USD 80 in 1991. Life expectancy at birth was 47 years, on a par with other war-torn countries. Infant mortality at 147 per 1000 live births was among the highest and primary school enrolment was only 41% while the illiteracy rate was 67%. RENAMO had destroyed over 700 schools during the civil-war. An article in Time magazine in 1992 stated that only fragile life-lines of emergency aid from abroad were keeping millions of people from dying of starvation.

The objective of the project was to improve the quality of primary education and this included some new and rehabilitated facilities at primary teachers training centres. These were currently ongoing so I had to report on their progress. Accompanied by personnel from the project office, we first flew to Beira, Sofala province about 1,000 km up the coast where we contacted the provincial education office. Beira had obviously seen better times and it felt strange searching to find a restaurant for lunch along the middle of a compact central area, almost deserted and with many windows broken each side. Beira was a RENAMO stronghold and had suffered during the war but one could see from the jacaranda and flame trees lining the streets that it must have been a very beautiful city before the war. We visited the Primary Teachers Training College, met all the operational parties including the contractor and the supervising architect Larisa from Russia, and did all that we were there to do.

We stayed there overnight and that evening, I was invited out to dinner by a resident Irish quantity surveyor to a seafood restaurant on the beach overlooking the Indian Ocean. It was great but they had few customers. Next morning at breakfast I met an interesting German engineer, there on behalf of the Deutsche Gesellschaft fur Technische Zusammenarbeit GTZ. They were financially assisting in the rehabilitation of Gorongosa National Park using the expertise from the adjoining Kruger Park in South Africa. Indeed the only people around seemed to be those engaged in development or humanitarian aid as there was a great deal of unexploded mines on minor roads outside Maputo. I have always found such unscheduled informal meetings very useful in learning of conditions relating to the construction industry locally and they give another context in which to assess official versions.

Next morning we flew over the Zambezi River delta to Quelimane, a few hundred km further North in Zambezia Province. Again one could see the remains of a more prosperous past when we visited the ongoing PTTC construction and met all the interested and operational personnel. The contractor was Brazilian-Portuguese, currently living over the border in Zimbabwe, having previously departed Mozambique and Angola to avoid wars. He was obviously pleased to be back working in Mozambique and had come over that morning in his own private 'plane. On learning that I had not seen the Victoria Falls, he asked if I could take a couple of days off and he would take me all-over. Unfortunately, as attractive and genuine as the offer was, I had to decline for many obvious reasons. We stayed that night at the Chuabo Hotel and next day we returned to Maputo.

Maputo since 1976, formerly Lourenco Marques, had the infrastructure of an attractive city with wide avenues lined with jacaranda, acacia and flamboyant trees, pavement cafes and colourful markets. There was an interesting modern pyramid-shaped circular church with 12 projecting triangular windows around the base quite close to the hotel which I visited on the Sunday. I have always found that the interpretation of the liturgy can be very revealing of local culture including their dancing and music.

There was a World Bank mission at the hotel at that same time in respect of a similar project, so I made a point of meeting their architect Luis Secco Larravide. He was Uruguayan from Montevideo and as we exchanged ideas on our projects, we found we had a lot in common. We compared our experiences and project problems and were able to collaborate on design standards, procurement procedures and implementation requirements. All this was very useful as one should expect the messages that each were giving to our respective Banks to be the same or similar.

Over the years it had struck me that the crime rate was invariably low at a time of political violence. Immediately after the end of the war, a strange calm prevails for a time and I have a few times experienced this as a very safe and peaceful time in a country. Certainly that was the situation existing during our mission to Mozambique but sadly the calm does not last. A couple of years later the travel advice of western governments in respect of Mozambique was that armed robbery was prevalent in Maputo so avoid walking down-town after dark. Theft of vehicles at gun-point was common with attacks unnecessarily vicious and occasionally fatal and for all journeys outside Maputo, travelling in convoy was strongly recommended. We left Maputo for a stopover of about six hours in Johannesburg waiting for a connecting flight to Abidjan where we were to prepare our report for the African Development Bank. I had no plans but was hoping to see something of Johannesburg. I had never been there but given all the warnings about the violent crime rate I was just trying to decide what I would do when I got talking to the passenger beside me.He lived in

Johannesburg and was returning from a business trip. When he heard my story he invited me to join him, he had a reliable taxi meeting him and after dropping him at his house, he would tell the driver a route to take me. I was delighted and we set off from Jan Smuts airport towards the city centre, then turned north and he pointed out the areas of interest. We passed Killarney and the Alexandra town-ship before reaching Sandton where he lived.

It was obviously a wealthy and professional area with lovely landscaped detached houses and I noted that security was a priority. I thanked him and set off with Dusan, the driver who had come to South Africa about 3 years earlier from Bosnia. When I asked about going to Soweto he said he had never been there so I realised I was to be taken on a sanitised tour which would exclude Soweto and all townships. We stopped at the Sandton Centre which was a huge modern mall beautifully set out on a number of floors and the complex included a luxury hotel. I spent some time there looking at the types of articles for sale and in many ways we could be in Europe or the United States. We then drove to the city centre to see the Bree and Commissioner shopping streets and impala fountain in Rissik Street before heading back to the airport.

We had a quick stop at Lome, Togo and I remembered being there thirty two years earlier in December 1961. During some local leave, Dympna and I had driven from Kaduna to Eastern Nigeria to Enugu and Onitsha and across the south to Lagos. On the way we stayed in a mission house in Enugu-Ezike where both topography and people were totally different from those in the North. We continued on along the coast through the Republic of Benin, Dahomey as it was then, to Lome where we stayed at Hotel du Golfe. We had been living in Nigeria eight months at that stage and were used to British protocols. We dressed that evening for dinner and came down to the cocktail bar. We were surprised to see a Frenchman sitting at the bar counter in shorts but "worse" was to follow, a Togolese arrived also in shorts to join the Frenchman, this would never happen at the Kaduna

Club where the only black African would be behind the bar counter. That was my first introduction to francophone Africa and after the initial shock, found it very refreshing. Indeed it is probably this ease of racial mix that best characterises the difference between the anglophone and francophone worlds.

Site personnel, Quelimane 1993   Old school friends Banjul Gambia 1975

COTE d' IVOIRE

I enjoyed my three visits for report writing in Abidjan. The African Development Bank headquarters is there and we stayed at the small French style Tiama Hotel, a walking distance from the Bank, in the central Plateau district.

I think the country is the personification of Felix Houphouet-Boigny, medical doctor, wealthy farmer,and son of a wealthy Baoule Chief. He became the first African Minister in the French Government and the first President of an independent Cote d'Ivoire in 1960. After WWII when other leaders like Kwame Nkruma and Sekou Toure were pushing for independence, he did not understand why they wanted it but given the option of independence within the French community by President de Gaulle, he accepted.

By maintaining the closest of links with France, the country presented a picture of sophistication and efficiency in the heart of Africa. The roads, hotels, tourist resorts and agricultural plantations were expanded with the active participation of the many French residents and large financial inputs from France

Houphouet-Boigny disliked the alphabetical confusion at international gatherings when the country was placed under "C" on French occasions, "I" when in the English language and "S" in Arabic so he declared the official name to be Cote d'Ivoire.

I was in Abidjan on a week-end in December 1993 when the death of the President was announced and Houphouet-Boigny's departure marked the end of an era for the Cote d' Ivoire. It has since experienced the volatile political uncertainties including military take-over in 1999, common to many African countries. In 1992 their economic and social indicators were considerably better than any of her West African neighbours but sadly they have been in decline since. Subsequent violence led to the AfDB move to Tunis but it returned when the war ended.

On one weekend, the Chadian leader of the mission to Mozambique, Miarro II took me to Grand Bassam, the first capital in the 1890s and now a pleasant seaside resort. It has charming old colonial buildings, many artisan stalls, a good beach and a number of ethnic restaurants.Yamoussoukro was the birthplace and last resting place of President Houphouet-Boigny and has been the political and administrative capital of the country since 1983. It is laid out in a "grand manner" and although there is much work to be completed it is a pleasant drive of some 200 km north of Abidjan. I went there particularly to see the remarkable Basilica of "Notre Dame de la Paix" which was consecrated by Pope John Paul II in 1990. The basilica, designed in the likeness of St. Peters in Rome complete with a similar esplanade, is a breathtaking sight virtually 'in the bush', with a superb dome, stained glass windows from France and multi-coloured Italian marble all set in formal gardens in the style of French palaces of the "Ancien Regeme". One can get a wonderful view of the city and Cathedral from the cantilevered restaurant on top of the Hotel President nearby.

Abidjan, the commercial and industrial capital with it's gleaming skyscrapers and modern buildings, stands in striking contrast to the run down capitals of some West African countries. On a hill at the north end of the Plateau area stands the very modern Cathedral of Saint Paul which has a capacity of 3,500 people. It is a very impressive original design facing the lagoon and with a backdrop of modern skyscrapers. The plan of the Cathedral is triangular and the bell-tower of three pillars stands firmly like a cross at the north end reminiscent of the Christ of Rio de Janeiro. From the tower, seven main stays supported by seven pre-stressed concrete beams hold the roof, flowing out like the veil of a wedding dress and resting on the perimeter walls. All the modern artwork was equally impressive and I was particularly attracted to the maybe 20 meters long stained-glass window representing the arrival of the first two missionaries at Grand Bassam in 1895.

Cathedral of Saint Paul, Abidjan Stained glass window depicting the arrival
Of the first white missionaries in 1895

One Sunday there was a special commemorative High-Mass at which there were two large choirs - one four-part of male and female voices and the other of women accompanied by traditional drums. The linking of the Latin liturgy with traditional African swaying rhythms, combining the French passion for aesthetic excellence and African natural ability for joyful celebration in that architectural setting was really wonderful and we were sorry when the ninety minute services finished.

On completion of the report at the Africa Development Bank headquarters in Cote d' Ivoire, consultants debrief at the UNESCO offices in Paris.

During my itinerant career I had always sought to keep in touch with Africa where that life started. The adaptation of the people: Tuaregs to the desert, Pygmies to the equatorial forest and Masai to the steppes seem to have a haunting appeal. The diversity of the people, culture and environment is always a source of wonder.

If I had not been back to Africa for 3-years, I would call to UNESCO for an assignment there. In my boyhood dreams of Africa, Kenya was the country I thought best represented my images of spacious landscapes, exotic wild animals and safari adventures, so when I applied to the British Colonial Office in 1959 I asked if it was possible to get a position in Kenya. I was informed that positions there were highly sought after and did not become available very often as appointees tended to stay.

KENYA

Kenya's prehistory began with the ancestors of homo-sapiens about 2.5 million years ago as confirmed by the Leakey studies and their excavations in the Rift Valley/Lake Turkana area. Throughout the ages, the coast was strongly influenced by Indian, Persian and Arab cultures which arrived in their dhows with the north-east monsoons, a fact already recorded in Roman times. In the 19th century German missionaries arrived followed by English trading companies and the construction of the Kenya-Uganda railway line opened the interior to the cultivation of the highlands by British settlers. The first national political movement was formed among the Kikuyu people in 1919, the aim was Freedom, Uhuru in Swahili, and Jomo Kenyatta became the important symbol. Independence was not achieved until 1963 and Mr. Kenyatta was elected the first President. He died in 1978 and his successor was still in power as we entered the 21st century and like many African leaders, he probably stayed too long.

Kenya is bisected horizontally by the Equator and vertically by the Great Rift Valley, a geological structure formed by the sinking of a strip of land between two parallel faults. Visible from a space the valley forms a 50 to 90 km wide trench down the length of Africa. Kenya is one of the most beautiful countries of the African Continent and the quintessential picture is of uncluttered spaciousness, laterite roads in golden, shimmering grassland with scattered baobab trees,all in the sun. It has variegated green hills and mountains in the hazy distance all under a clear royal blue sky.

The National Parks commenced in 1946 with the first on the outskirts of Nairobi and since then countless reserves have been established to preserve Kenya's unique wildlife. They are not zoos but great tracts of wilderness set aside for preservation of flora and fauna, open during daylight hours and policed by rangers. In these parks, animals have the right-of-way, they become aggressive if cut off from water hole or a mother separated from her young. One never gets out of a vehicle when approaching an animal and doors and windows remain closed.

Like all new democracies, Kenya has experienced ups and downs since independence and was in a difficult period of decline as the indicators in the World Bank annual atlas indicate:

1961 – Population estimated at 6.5 million

1984 – Population 19.5 ml - per capita GNP $310
    Life expectancy 54 yrs

1991 - Population 25.8 ml - per capita GNP $340
Life expectancy 59 yrs - Illiteracy 31%

1996 - Population 27.3 ml - per capita GNP $320
Life expectancy 58 yrs

My first trip to Kenya was in 1984 for an United Nations Development Program project. It involved four days of meetings at the United Nations Center for Human Settlements (Habitat) in the Kenyatta International Conference Center in Nairobi. I did not see a great deal but did visit the

Parliament Buildings, Law Courts and the Holy Family Cathedral where I noted many Irish names. I was able to spend a few hours in the Nairobi National Park where, only 8 km from the city center, wildlife is abundant and I was able to see giraffe, buffalo, zebra, lion, various antelopes, etc. in their natural setting. The park is unique in it's location on the threshold of a major city and conserves an un-spoilt tract of forest, woodland and grassland of about 120 square kilometers.

Four years later, Dympna and I visited Kenya 'on safari' where everything one sees is spontaneous and authentic. There is no question of situations being "put-on" for the tourist. We arrived in Monbasa, an old trading city of visiting dhows and the chief port of the country. Built on an island for reasons of security around a natural harbor with an intriguing area of tightly packed 19th century housing, it had grown to become the center for the very popular coastal holidays.

After a quick tour of the city we drove to the Tsavo East National Park and checked into the Voi Safari Lodge. Tsavo is a superb wilderness of endless plains and volcanic hills traversed by two rivers, which are essential for wildlife. It is Kenya's largest national park at over 8,000 square km varying in height from 230 to 2,000 meters above sea level. We were taken around the park in a four-wheel drive minibus with high ground clearance and good viewing space including roof hatches to 'shoot' all we were lucky to see with cameras. For me, the sight of the graceful giraffe eating the high young leaves of the eucalyptus trees and running in a wavelike motion was particularly memorable.

Our bedroom overlooked a watering pool and during the night, Dympna woke me to see a pride of seven white lions quietly drinking in the moonlight. Next day we arrived at the Ngulia Lodge in Tsavo West and went to see the hippo having their evening bath in the Mzima springs. Arriving at the Kilimanjaro Safari Lodge next day, the ever abiding memory I have of the Amboseli National Park is of sitting outside on a terrace before sunset, drinking a tusker lager and watching a large herd of elephant strolling by the lakeside and zebra grazing nearby with the awe-inspiring ice-crowned summit of Mount Kilimanjaro towering in the background.

Streams rising in the mountain reappear in the center of the park to create verdant swamps that support a rich diversity of wild animals and bird-life so that rattling across open grassland from observation hills to swamps to see the wildlife eating, sleeping, fighting, bathing or doing nothing at all was an exciting experience.

We stopped for a few days in Nairobi which, started as a railhead before becoming the center of colonial East-Africa. We went north to the Aberdare National Park in the highlands. On the way we visited Thikaand Nyeri where we had lunch at the well known Outspan Hotel.

Kenya, Amboseli Park and Mount Kilmanjaro, Tanzania

That night we stayed at the unique night game-viewing Treetops Lodge, literally a raw three storey timber building first built as a simple tree-house in 1932, burnt down in 1954 and rebuilt a few years later. The water-hole and area around was floodlit, which did not seem to bother the animals, and through the night we saw about a dozen different species from rhino to warthog. The wire netting on the open bedroom windows was essential to keep the monkeys out because they seem to spend their time climbing up looking for food. There was a bell in each room which would ring whenever there was any special wildlife activity. There too we were in the delightful company of Josie MacAvin from Dublin, who won an Oscar for the Set Decoration of the film "Out of Africa" and she entertained us with her tales from the film set.

In the morning we had coffee there before returning to the Outspan hotel for breakfast on the terrace in the beautiful gardens with the snow capped Mount Kenya as a backdrop. They like to tell visitors of the world renowned guests who have stayed at Treetops over the years and they are particularly proud of the young English girl who arrived with her husband in February 1952, she climbed into the tree one evening as a Princess and came down the next morning as Queen Elizabeth II.

I was very pleased to be invited again in February 1997 by UNESCO who act as agent for the African Development Bank, to join an AfDB double supervision mission to Kenya and Mauritius. Working in a country on projects in the social sector is a privileged way of meeting the people as it gives a deeper insight to their way of life. I was briefed at the UNESCO Headquarters in Paris before proceeding on the mission. The objective of the Education Project was to improve the quality of the education and training system in a work and development oriented direction. It comprised the design, construction, furnishing and equipping of a new Primary Teacher Training College in the western province, the rehabilitation of 15 existing PTTCs, science equipment for over a thousand schools, facility maintenance and support for technical education.

My terms of reference were to review with each of the relevant ministries, all aspects of the civil works component from initiation to completion including arrangements for future maintenance, the work-program and compliance with Bank requirements. I had therefore to work closely with the officials at the ministries some of whom accompanied me on the field-trips.

Returning to the slow city traffic of Nairobi in the evening was always hazardous. The many urchins of 10 to 14 years were ready to snatch articles from vehicles and break windows if an opportunity was seen. One mid-day an urchin grabbed our mission leader's handbag when Kadija was out on her own, there was a tug-of-war which luckily she won but she did get a fright. That evening we treated her to dinner at an Italian restaurant, the nationality of her husband, to offset any nervousness remaining.

Our first field-trip was to see the Teacher Training Institute at Thika, a fine old Colonial-style stone building built in the 1950s and well suited to upgrading in the project. There was a similar facility at Kabete which we visited on the way to Bungoma in the Western Province near the Uganda border. Shortly after leaving Nairobi, we had a wonderful panoramic view of the Rift Valleyfrom the edge of the escarpment to the hazy mountains in the distance before we dropped about 600 meters to the floor of the valley. We were now entering the onetime heart of the White Highlands.

Mission *crossing the Equator* 1997   *The Kenyatta Centre, Nairobi*

On the way too we passed three of the central lakes, famous as a paradise for bird-watchers where the lakes are home to millions of flamingos, which tint their alkaline waters a deep pink. The lakes are unusual in that none of them has an obvious outflow, water pours in from the surrounding countryside, evaporation keeps the levels constant but two of the lakes are so saline that they are virtually undrinkable.

Lake Naivasha is a freshwater lake surrounded by very fertile agricultural land where one can expect to see hippo and buffalo in the swamps on the north side. Joy Adamson's Elsamere Center of "Born Free" fame is on the south side. Further on we passed Lakes Elmenteita and Nakuru, noted for their flamingo dappled waters and great white pelicans, but can vary greatly in area and almost dried up entirely in the 1950s. Between Nakuru and Eldoret we passed the sign noting our position on the Equator.

We rose out of the valley near Eldoret and continuing west where the horizon was dominated by the extinct volcano Mount Elgon which seemed so near later when we stopped at Kibabii, north of Bungomo, to discuss all the arrangements for the construction of the new PTTC with the contractor.

The site was large enough to allow for future development, the contours were suitable for drainage, utilities were available, soil test results were satisfactory, the contractor was setting up his stores and site arrangements so everything looked good to proceed. We stayed overnight at the forest area of Kakamega, 1930s center of gold-mining and returned the 300 km by the same route next day.

With the implementation arrangements and progress of the project all in order, the wrap-up meetings were completed over the following couple of days and the aide-memoire agreed for Government and Bank records. As I prepared to depart, I thought it was not surprising that in those days gone-by, when a person got a job in Kenya, they were inclined to stay.

THE CONGO

For each of the projects in Africa, financed by the AfDB, we started in Paris and ended in Abidjan before returning to Paris. There are very limited schedules across Africa so to get from East to West we invariably traveled from Nairobi to Abidjan by Ethiopian Airways, making a number of stops on the way.

After the Kenyan mission we stopped at Brazzaville, Congo. It seemed strange that this low-rise city had been the Capital of French equatorial Africa and General de Gaulle had made it the Capital of Free France for a time during WWII. The quiet provincial appearance contrasted sharply with the skyscraper city of Kinshasa across the river. My flying companion was returning to the city and I asked if he crossed to Kinshasa often but he smiled and said, very rarely as there were problems between the two countries. John Gunther in "Inside Africa" states that parrots in considerable numbers cross the river from Brazzaville each morning and return every evening but nobody knows why.

On another occasion, we stopped atKinshasa for security reasons. This seemed ironic because I had always considered Kinshasa to be one of the most volatile and dangerous places in Africa. On landing we were told to stay on board and we would be off again in less than an hour. The hour passed and as it became two, an uneasiness started to creep through the airplane. After a further 45 minutes, relief as the engines started and after a further 15 minutes we were drawn back from the stand and turned towards the taxi-way for take-off we assumed but nothing happened. Another 45 minutes we started moving again but to our dismay we returned to the stand and the engines were turned off. Another hour passed and the uneasiness turned to anxiety as rumors floated through the airplane; someone important was arriving and we were to be taken to the city by bus. Finally after a further 30 minutes the engines started, excitement passed through the aircraft and in 20 minutes we were ascending to our to 35,000 feet, not a foot too little and towards our next stop, Lome en route to Abidjan. We learned unofficially that the delay occurred because of an altercation between the Captain who spoke English and the Traffic controller who spoke French. I made a decision that the next time I crossed Africa my route would be Nairobi - Paris - Abidjan by Air France.

UGANDA

Next stop was another former problem area as later in 1997. I was asked by UNESCO to join another Af DB supervision mission, this time to Uganda and I was pleased to be able to continue my travels further westward into Africa. The verdant hills around Lake Victoria were "darkest Africa" to Europeans in 1862 when English explorer John Speke went seeking the source of the Nile. A decade later, following an exploratory visit by the US American explorer Henry Stanley, Missionaries and British traders began arriving and settling in Uganda. After a negotiated Anglo-German treaty, Uganda formally became a British Protectorate in 1894 with Entebbe as the capital. Nationalist parties developed after WWII and Uganda became an independent nation in 1962 with Dr Milton Obote as Prime Minister in a climate of great promise. Its position seemed assured, as one of the most prosperous and well managed states in East Africa, but culturally divided, the euphoria did not last. In 1971 the notorious Idi Amin seized power in a military coup. He declared an economic war, deported most Asians who had been the pillar of the commercial society and Uganda went into a severe decline. The economy dried-up, buildings were not maintained, unrest and instability led to looting and rioting. Businesses closed or cut-back leading to a lack of raw materials, goods and services. The city population grew as young people moved from rural areas in search of work and a better life. Amin invaded Tanzania in 1978 and as a result fell in 1979 to an alliance of opposition forces leading to the return of Obote. He changed the constitution to a Presidential system and promptly set out to remove opponents. This led to the indiscriminate slaughter of thousands in the Luwero Triangle.

It was only when Yoweri Museveni came to power in 1986 and set out to revitalize the economy with the assistance of the World Bank and other international donors that the country began to improve.

Unfortunately with other countries from East to Southern Africa, it was then hit by the appalling plague of HIV/AIDs which in Uganda spread heterosexually and affected both sexes. These facts are reflected in the economic indicators which show the per capita GNP rise from 1984 when there were no figures available to $ 170 in 1991 and $ 300 in 1996 but the social indicators show a tragic pattern in the opposite direction: life expectancy at birth went from 51 years in 1984 to 46 years in 1992 and 43 years in 1996 while child malnutrition went up from 23% in 1992 to 26% in 1996.

The approach to the international airport at Entebbi, gateway and first capital, is very impressive as one sweeps across the great expanse of Lake Victoria, the second largest freshwater lake in the world. Unfortunately with bilharzia endemic it cannot be used for recreation as one might like. However, Uganda, with natural beauty and wildlife attractions, was a very popular tourist destination until Amin came to power. We traveled the 35 km by minibus to the capital Kampala and the hotel in the city centre was impressively situated on top of a hill with good views over the entire city.

The projectobjective was to strengthen the science and technical teaching capacity in Kampala and Kyambogo. My time wasmostly in the project office in Kampala and the facilities to be inspected were within a 20 km radius. We first visited Makerere University, to see theScience and Technology renovations provided and equipped under the project.

Nearby are the Kasubi Tombs where a huge circular thatched building, a good example of traditional architecture, houses the tombs of the late kings of Buganda who had died between 1884 and 1966. I als visit some of the important religious buildings including the Catholic Rubaga with some good stained glass windows and the Anglican Namirembe Cathedrals as well as the Kibuli Mosque.

We inspected the Uganda Polytechnic and Institute of Teacher Education, about 10 km north-east to see the rehabilitation works at the two institutions. We also visited the Uganda Martyrs Secondary School and Greenhill Academy and went on to see the Namugongo Shrines which commemorate the martyrdom of the first Christians, canonised by Pope John Paul II and visited by him in 1993. The significance of the shrine was brought home to me when I thought of what my Zairean colleague had told me during our trip across Nigeria in 1989.

The mission on the whole was not one of my more memorable so I was very glad of the good spirits of my Kenyan colleague Kilemi Mwiria. Over a week-end we went to Jinji, 80 km east at the head of Napoleon Gulf passing the Owen Falls Dam, the hydroelectric development that has generated power for the entire country and parts of Kenya and Tanzania since 1952. Jinji also features the apparent but contentious Source of the Nile where Lake Victoria empties into the White Nile and begins it's 6,400 km journey through the Sudan and Egypt to the Mediterranean Sea.

LESOTHO

Lesotho, previously Basutoland, emerged as a single entity in 1822. Moshoeshoe, a son of a minor chief of the Bakoteli lineage, formed his own clan and became a chief around 1804. Between 1821 and 1823, he and his followers settled in the mountains and joined with former adversaries in resistance to those associated with the Zulu Kingdom from 1818 to 1828.

Examples of Art of the World

In 1854 the British pulled out of the region and in 1858 Moshoeshoe fought a series of wars with the Boers, losing a great portion of the western lowlands. The last war in 1867 ended when Moshoeshoe appealed to Queen Victoria, who agreed to make Basutoland a British protectorate in 1868. In 1869, the British signed a treaty with the Boers that defined the boundaries of Basutoland which by ceding the western territories effectively reduced Moshoeshoe's kingdom to half its previous size.

In 1869 the British initially transferred functions from Moshoeshoe's capital to a police camp at Maseru, until administration of Basutoland was transferred to the Cape Colony in 1871. Moshoeshoe died in 1870, marking the end of the traditional era and the beginning of the colonial era.

Between 1871 and 1884, Basutoland was treated similarly to territories that had been forcefully annexed, much to the chagrin of the people of Basotho. This led to war again in 1881. In 1884, Basutoland was restored in status to a protectorate, with Maseru ascapital. It remained under direct rule by a governor, though effective internal power was wielded by traditional chiefs. In 1966

Basutoland gained independence as the Kingdom of Lesotho.

In 2002 I was invited to join the Boston University, Center for International Health Team that was appointed to carry out an Economic Study of the Referral Health Services in Lesotho. The study was also to include recommendations for the future of the Queen Elizabeth II Hospital in the capital, Maseru. The team below included the late William Bicknell who had played a large part in the formation of the currentUniversity School of Public Health.

I was responsible for civil works component including the terms of reference for the new hospital to replace the Queen Elizabeth II.
I subsequently learned that the new Queen 'Mamohato Memorial Hospital, which we recommended in 2002, was completed and officially opened in October 2011.

The team relaxing at the end of the week

New Hospital Maseru 2011

Boston University Mission Brief 2002

MAURITIUS

Flying out from Paris where I was briefed in 1997 for a double mission to Mauritius and Kenya, we stopped at the Seychelles en route. Approaching and depating we got very good views of the main Mahe Island. About 26 km long by 7 km wide, Mahe is a large granite island, 4 degrees south of the Equator, covered in dense tropical forest and vegetation. The runway on which we landed was close to and parallel with the shore. The terminal was a small single storey building with only space for the access road parallel to the shore and the mountains rose sharply.

The Seychelles has an history similar to Mauritius but smaller mountainous and unsuitable for agriculture. Tourism is a major industry although they limit the numbers to protect the environment and their way of life. There is an abundance of flora, bird and marine life and with no poisonous snakes, malarial mosquitoes and little crime, it is a place I would like to return.

We spent one week in Mauritius, two weeks in Kenya and two weeks report writing at the AfDB headquarters in Abidjan. Mauritius, lying 2,000 km off the coast of Africa in the Indian Ocean, was an uninhabited island until France started a colonial society in 1721. The British took control in 1810 and with intensive sugar cane cultivation new sources of labor were required. They came from South Asia and by 1860 were 65% of the total population. Stagnating investment and rising unemployment in the 20th century heightened tensions between the communities leading to a movement towards independence which was fulfilled in 1968. A Republic was declared in 1992.

Although the French period was only 90 years and the British over 150 years, the culture of the people is predominantly French and both languages are used throughout including the Parliament. Mauritius or Ile Maurice was a classic example of a one crop country with tourism growing to number two. In 1996 the World Bank economic table placed their per capita GNP at the 42nd position in the world of 157 countries listed and their social indicators placed them just behind the developed world countries.

The objectives of the project were to improve access to education through the development of a distance education capacity. It included courses for upgrading primary school teachers, science and technology teaching staff and the facilities at secondary schools. Like most such projects, it also had a maintenance and repair strategy component for buildings andequipment. I inspected the laboratory and workshops at the Mauritius Institute of Education and a new media and resource center at the Mauritius College of the Air. I found the creation of such a multimedia center with capacity for producing printed, aural, visual still and moving picture interactive training packages available to computer stations at schools a wonderful state-of-the-art development.

I remembered Stan Scheyer, a public health specialist, having a hard time trying to promote similar concepts for the dissemination of medical and health awareness programs in the Philippines. We also visited other facilities in the Capital which were linked to twenty secondary schools.

Port Louis the capital was a busy city port and most activity was concentrated there but Mauritius Island is only about 70 km by 50 km so visiting the project sites was not a problem. The College of the Air,the State School at Belle Rose and JFK College at Beau Bassam wereup on the plateau, a very desirable residential area. Curepipe too, 600 meters above sea level with some French colonial buildings, is particularly attractive and there is a scenic drive along the rim of the Trou aux Cerfs crater above the town.

We stayed at the Maritim Hotel overlooking Turtle Bay on the West coast.We stood out work in our "uniform" of long trousers and tie. We took the opportunity of visiting the Pamplemousses Gardens, where they had a large collection of indigenous and exotic plants, well known to naturalists for the variety of palm trees. Following our wrap-up meeting we departed to our next mission before reporting back to the AfDB Headquarters.

PAPUA NEW GUINEA

PNG with New Ireland, Bird of Paradise and Southern Cross

From the Indian Ocean I went to the Pacific Ocean to PNG.

During my years as an itinerant architect, I kept meeting consultants who spoke of their experiences in Papua New Guinea as being in a very special category. I developed a great curiosity about the place so in 1998 when I was invited to participate in a supervision mission of a Primary Health Care project there, I was particularly delighted to accept. Because of the well published activities of the notorious "rascals", I asked the mission leader Maria McDonald at the World Bank if the country was safe. A wonderful Dutch woman with a great sense of humor, she assured me that she would mind me, so off I went reassured!

As I got to the boarding gate on my way from London to Brisbane, the stewardess told me that they were upgrading me to first class travel. Accordingly, I had my British Airways bed and they even gave me a "first class" pyjamas so I arrived 23 hours later fully refreshed and there I stayed some 36 hours adjusting to the time-change before carrying on to join the mission at Port Moresby.

Brisbane grew from an original penal settlement in the 19th century to it's present 1.5 million and is built on a river which plays an important part in the outdoor lifestyle of the residents in this sub-tropical city. I stayed at an international hotel in the center of town from which after such a long flight, I walked a lot around the city. I seem to have a passion for Botanical Gardens and here they were conveniently nearby. I took a boat trip on the Brisbane River to get the flavour of the Indooroopilly golf club and called to St. Stephen's Cathedral because I understood it to have a distinct Irish ambiance.

PNG has had a fascination for foreigners because it was viewed as a mysterious and exotic land untouched by modern life where stories abound of lost tribes and head-hunters, untouched by modern life and still living on traditional hunting and gathering,. The rugged mountainous Pacific island north-east of Australia comprises two main territories. The western half is Irian Jaya Indonesia, formerly Dutch New Guinea and the eastern half together with a group of smaller islands is PNG which before the First World War was divided between German New Guinea in the north and British Papua in the south. After the war in 1920, the League of Nations gave PNG to Australia as a mandated territory. It had experienced fierce fighting both there and in the Solomon Islands during WWII after which Australia continued to administer the territory until Independence in 1975. About that time one newspaper held a competition for a more appropriate or shorter name for the country and first prize was won by a 10 year-old girl from Port Moresby with the suggestion "Niugini". However, "Papua New Guinea" remained but the airline adopted the winning name "Air Niugini".

The people are mainly Melanesian but divided by impenetrable mountain vegetation. They have great linguistic diversity with about 800 distinct languages spoken, making it a Pacific Tower of Babel. The lingua franca is Pidgin English and the variant used is Tok Pisin, for example when I did not want to be disturbed, I hung the following notice outside the door - "plis noken mekim nois". It has been said that there are some 5,000 languages in daily use throughout the world and over 15% of those are spoken in PNG alone. Each linguistic group or "wontok" has its' own traditions and sense of identity. Most people live by subsistence farming in villages so they are not badly off but settlements can vary from a few huts to communities of a couple of thousand people and traditionally each had little contact with those outside their own area, whom they often regarded with hostility or fear. The diversity of the terrain, impenetrable forest, towering mountains and coastal swamps, no doubt contributed to the isolation of each group and reinforced their strong sense of cultural identity.

Politics in PNG too are unusual in that the party system is very weak and "crossing the floor" is commonplace as politicians jump from party to party. Since independence, no government has gone full term, most having been brought down by votes of "no confidence". In 1991 the Constitution was even amended prohibiting the tabling of such motions for eighteen months of a new government's term, previously the threshold was six months after which they could fall any day. In one sense they have too much democracy but in spite of all the predictions of gloom, they have survived.

The project aimed to improve primary health care, reduce the population growth rate and crude death rate by increasing the number of outpatient clinical outlets. The project was well advanced so we were to inspect as many facilities as possible to ensure compliance with the project objectives as appraised and agreed some years earlier. Each of the mission members visited different provinces, Danielle Tronchet to the Eastern Highlands, Maria took the Western Highlands, I went to the Southern Highlands and flew to Mendi with Homolpi Warom from the Department. Flying over PNG, one is struck by the density and mass of forests that cover the country. In fact almost 90% of the land-mass is covered and they have always been one of Papua New Guinea's most valuable resource.

The highlands were the last part of the country to be explored by Europeans who did not encounter the people there until the 1930s. Up to that time it was generally thought the people only lived in the coastal plains and the largely inaccessible mountain regions were uninhabited. In fact the highlands were the most densely populated but it was not until the 1950s and 1960s after WWII, that they were discovered.

There are only two road systems, one on the south coast with the capital Port Moresby at the center, in total about 400 km. The other, the north coast highway stretches about 400 km from Lae, off which a highland road was added to Mount Hagan in the Eastern Highlands and later extended to Mendi and eventually to Tari. The people of these highlands are famous for their ostentatious traditional dress including headdress, wigs and personal colourful decoration to face and bodies. The Southern Highlands are the most remote and are still relatively undeveloped. Accordingly, one must fly from one area to another and then use the local road system. I spent a few days in Mendi and was obliged to stay an extra day as an expected earlier flight failed to arrive because of morning fog.

The town is small and built around the airport but it had the very pleasant Kiburu Lodge on 30 acres just outside town, built in traditional chalets with thatched roofs, beside a mountain river amongst the lush alpine rain forests of the Mendi valley. There we stayed enclosed by

159

security fencing as we dined to a cacophony of sounds of water and wildlife.

For historic reasons, the implementation of the civil works in that particular province was the responsibility of the Australian army and Warrant Officer Arnold Fox was the Senior Works Superintendent dealing with the project. He was new and was also in charge of the entertainment at the army mess so invariably we ended at the mess each evening. A couple of his local staff accompanied us on our field-trips from Magarina in the north-west, near Tari, to Ialibu, about halfway to Mount Hagan in the Eastern Highlands.

On one occasion we were stopped on the road by locals who claimed they had filled the pot-holes and wanted us to pay them before we could proceed. Luckily one of the men from the Mendi office with us had the same "wontok" and convinced them we had no money with us. He negotiated a settlement for some bananas, peanuts and bread-rolls which we had with us for sustenance. Before leaving Mendi we agreed a program for works completion as the Australian Army were due to withdraw in 1999 and we hoped all works would be finished before their departure. The Highland countryside was very remote but with the Australian army protecting me I had no worries and enjoyed the few days enormously.

Returning to Port Moresby where we stayed in the Travelodge at Waigani, close to the Government Offices, we visited some clinics at Tokorara and Gordons with John Paton, a New Zealand architect whose practice had previously been engaged by the Department on some of the work. His wife too ran a private clinic which was well worth seeing in respect of the standards that could be achieved. We went into the town-center a few times and I found an art store where I got an interesting sculptured "headhunter" as a souvenir. Hanuabada village on stilts on the shore is very picturesque but we were advised against going into it. The simple Parliament building and particularly the artwork above the entrance was very beautiful.

On the Saturday we visited Loloata Island in Bootless Bay about 20 km from Port Moresby for an afternoon, where the eco-system contains just about every major habitat, from mangroves to sea-grass meadows and coral reefs and it was home to the most beautiful, bizarre and bewitching marine creatures. There I practiced snorkeling in preparation for the Great Barrier Reef. Having come from the original too, I was sorry I was unable to visit the island of New Ireland.

Sydney Opera House   Uluru (Ayres Rock)   Barrier Reef

Following the wrap-up and completion of our PNG reports in 1998, I departed for Cairns in Queensland, Australia. It was only an hour from Port Moresby so I was well settled before Dympna joined me next morning for a holiday in Australia. It struck me that this was one of the few tropical countries where on arrival I did not have to worry about the selection of a taxi or the advance negotiation of a fare. It is a wonderful Continent for a holiday and in 3-weeks we visited the tourist triangle of Great Barrier Reef, Red Center and Sydney where I fulfilled an ambition by attending a concert at the Sydney Opera House which I have considered to be one of the outstanding architectural works of the 20th century.

The Great Barrier Reef is certainly one of our planet's greatest natural attractions and the abundance of species and their ecological complexity are enormous. Coral reefs derive their primary energy from solar radiation and thrive between the latitudes 30 degrees north to 30 degrees south where water temperatures coincide with an optimum 20 degrees Centigrade. Reefs can vary in formation from coastal or island fringing to platform or barrier reefs and successive layers of living coral grow around the fringe of a volcanic island, as it gradually sinks, resulting in the formation of an atoll. Marine plants including algae, sea-weeds and sea-grasses are the basic food and provide nutrition for the multitude of microorganisms as well as molluscs, crustaceans and fish. On the reef one can see a multitude of life forms including single cell, sponges, jellyfish, corals, marine worms, crustaceans from shrimps, barnacles, crabs, clams to lobsters, sea shells, nudibranchs, starfish, sea urchins, squirts and a multitude of fish, octopus, sea snakes and turtles. The variety and color of each species is staggering so that even a first time snorkler can be overwhelmed by the parade of exotic life forms in front of them.

One could not but be impressed at how careful Australia is of their environment. Visitors were discouraged from walking on the coral for fear of damage. Boardwalks too were provided too at Daintree to avoid walking on the forest floor and when building the cable-car over the forest at Kuranda, they did so using helicopters to protect the forest. As I familiarized myself with Cairns that first evening, I met an US American couple at the Pier Marketplace that I had seen earlier on the flight from Port Moresby. They were on a cruising holiday around Australia. They mentioned that their tourist visa had expired after six months so they flew to PNG that morning to get a foreign stamp on their passport. They could then re-enter Australia anew in the afternoon to continue their retirement holiday for another six months. If Australia was only 6-hours flying time from home, I'm sure we would be there regularly.

Australia was the last great landmass to be colonized by Europeans and was only "discovered" for Britain in the 18th century. It quickly became their penal colony to which they exported convicts from their jails together with "political dissidents" from Ireland. From this harsh beginning, Australia evolved over the following 2-centuries in a similar way to the USA to become part of the developed world of to-day.

However, the native Aborigines still have more in common with the peoples of the developing world of Asia. Their economic and social circumstance including incomes, employment, housing, life expectancy, morbidity and infant mortality are similar.

From earlier prejudices and injustices, acknowledged finally by the Government in the 1990s, they are only now starting to emerge with their human rights recognized. About a quarter of the Aborigines live in the Northern Territories and it was flying to Alice Springs that we became aware of the immensity of the Continent. As we crossed the bridge to our hotel, we were told that beneath was the usually dry Todd River. A definition of a native of Alice is one who has seen the river flowing. Two hours later, to the astonishment of visitors and residents alike the river was suddenly in flood from upcountry rains fallen a few days earlier. Apparently it only happens about every seven years.

We drove south from Alice some 200 km and passed some huge ranches. At the entrance gate to one, a signpost advised that the avenue to the ranch was 70 km. We continued our trip to Uluru, the sacred rock of the Aborigines called Ayres Rock. Its colours change at sunset suddenly likea live ember so it was not surprising that the land has a spiritual value for the Aborigines. We later visited the Maruku gallery, established to encourage and support the Aboriginal craftspeople of the central and western desert regions. In this way they ensure the continuation of ancient skills in traditional and contemporary forms by selling their works to provide much needed income for the family groups in the region.

In this sparsely populated country I remembered the views of the taxi driver who had collected me at Cairns airport. He had emigrated from Britain some years earlier and had very strong views about most things, in particular he did not approve of all the Asians coming to the country. I thought the contrasting population densities between Asia and Australia made the flow of migrants from Asia inevitable. Australia was adapting itself to a new multicultural community and as a part of Asia. During my last mission to the Philippines in the autumn of 1997 and at a reception in the house of a Dutch colleague, Steven van der Tak, I was lucky to meet Patricia Moser an American who invited me to join a mission she planned the following Spring to Kyrgyzstan. Although I was not quite sure where exactly it was I said yes immediately and looked forward to my first trip to Central Asia.

CENTRAL ASIA

Central AsiaTraditional YURT   *In Kyrgyzstan with Patricia*

Central Asia incorporates the areas of the former Soviet Kazak, Uzbek, Kyrgyz, Tajik and Turkmen Republics as well as Xinjiang, Western China. It is a vast land north of the Himalayan ranges, with temperatures varying from -30 in winter to +30 degrees C in summer. Having arrived by air from Europe and although accustomed to spaciousness in Africa, it was on the drive from Almaty to Bishkek that I became conscious of the immensity of the Eurasian steppe which stretches across the globe from Hungary to Mongolia. Peoples, conquerors and cultures have crossed these steppes, deserts and mountains for thousands of years and one becomes aware of the sweep of history.

The vastness of the plain to the north, east and west, of fertile treeless grassland was emphasised during the 250 km drive by the snow-covered Alps-like Tian-Shan range bordering China to the south. This steppe has served as the highway and grazing ground for the nomadic peoples who can still be seen living in their yurt - the traditional cylindrical wood-framed insulated tent - riding the plains on horseback and wearing exotic hats or kalpaks.

From the 4th century of Alexander the Great to the 13th of Jenghis Khan to the 19th of the Russian Tsars, Central Asia has experienced the pendulum-like shifts of power between the nomadic hordes.

The 19th century saw Imperialist Russia extend its zone of influence into the area after centuries of this "the sweep of history" across the region which was not clearly defined. The present frontiers in Central Asia were set in a very arbitrary manner by the Soviet Border Commission in the 1920s, when new provisional governments were set-up. Bukhara and Samarkand were and are predominantly Tajik but in order to prevent those cities being included in the new Tajik SSR, the Uzbeks made Samarkand their capital. A little later, when there was talk of making Tashkent the capital of the Kazak SSR, they moved the capital to Tashkent and Almaty became the Kazak capital until 1997.

This heart of Central Asia is so empty and remote that it served as a convenient area for the setting up of a network of gulag labour camps for unwanted subjects from Dostoevsky to Solzhenitsyn and even for whole peoples disliked by Stalin. Hidden here too was the USSR's nuclear testing zone and main space launching centre. The whole area was closed-off to all foreigners throughout the 20th century until the collapse of the USSR and birth of the present five Central Asian Republics in 1991.

We flew to Almaty in Kazakstan, which is essentially a Russian city where they still make up the majority of the population. It was the capital until October 1997 when the government moved to Aqmola, far to the north. Aqmola was later renamed Astana.

Almaty is a modern clean park-land cosmopolitan model city of 1.5 million people as most of the old buildings were destroyed by the1911 earthquake One of the few buildings remaining from the tsarist-era is the beautiful Zenkov Cathedral, built in 1904 entirely of wood and without any nails.

Plastered and colourfully painted it was used during the soviet-era as a museum, a concert hall and then it was boarded-up until it was returned to the Orthodox Church in 1995. Apart from the building itself, the unique Orthodox art-form of iconostasis and icons around the cathedral were well worth the visit to see how the Orthodox Church uses iconography to explain theological precepts. There were no taxis in Almaty, you just stand by the side of the street and raise your hand. When a local private car stops, you negotiate a price for where you want to go and he will take you if the direction suits him. In this way I did the tourist highlights of the city.

Cathedral Almaty   *UN Convoy Dushambe*

KYRGYZSTAN

Kyrgyzstan is a beautiful country of snow-covered mountains known as the "Switzerland" of Central Asia. Although nomadic until almost the 20th century, medieval Kyrgyz was a crossroads on the Great Silk Road. It was on the great caravan route from China through Persia to the Mediterranean and became one of the cultural centres of the ancient Turkic nations. Along this route came Jenghis Khan and the Mongol Horde, sacking existing empires beyond and creating new ones for his family at romantic sounding places like Bukhara, Khiva and Samarkand, where his descendant Tamerlane ruled.

While Kyrgyzstan lacks a settled history, its literature has traditionally been popularised in song, poems, stories and oral legends by itinerant minstrels. Bishkekthe capital, previously called Frunze after a Russian General, is a friendly low-rise city of pleasant buildings, sculptured parks, tree-lined avenues, a snow-covered mountain backdrop and a population of about 700,000 of Russians, Kyrgyz and others. It seemed "provincial" compared to Almaty. Most of the Russians were Christian Orthodox religion so a couple of us set-off to the Russian Orthodox Cathedral one Sunday. The Orthodox Divine Liturgy was much longer than the Catholic Mass and for much of the Ordinary the priest is unseen behind the iconostasis, only appearing through the Royal Doors for Communion. Although hidden from view, there was continuous participation in the liturgy by the laity through plain chant responses with the celebrant. There were no seats or kneelers and the congregation stood or walked around to pray at their favourite icon. Kyrgyzstan was a communist country so we were surprised to see the church so completely packed. I called back another day to examine the architectural detail in the Cathedral and the priest, without any English or I Russian, very kindly took me around to show me the future improvements which he proudly proposed. In one hall there was a nine meter long roll of detail paper with designs of cherubim and seraphim as a template with which painters were engaged to cover the ceiling.

Towards the end of my final visit to Bishkek, I learned that there was a small Catholic church somewhere in the suburbs which I eventually found with difficulty. The happy outcome was that I was asked if I would prepare a design for a new church for Bishkek. In April 2000 I submitted a sketch design based on the traditional yurt and my proposal was enthusiastically received. Perhaps I may have the pleasure of returning one day to assist with its implementation and that would be a wonderful experience. The process however is not an easy one as the Catholic Church has first to be registered as a religious body in this Islamic country. That could take some time. It also has to obtain the necessary planning permits for construction of the church on the land and this can also take some time particularly if there are any objections which are quite possible. The Orthodox Church for one might not like the competition and their relations are not good since the break between Rome and Byzantium some 1000 years ago.

Bishkek has a fine theatre, museum, philharmonic hall, university and institutes as well as an opera house where La Traviata was playing while we were there and a Russian group was coming to the circus building the following week. A feature of all Former Soviet Union (FSU) countries was the emphasis on theatre, ballet and classical music at outrageously cheap prices e.g. what might cost 50 Euro in Europe or US would cost about 50 cents and always to full houses.

Travel books generally advise caution in the cities after dark but during our first mission in Bishkek, we were not aware of any special dangers. In the evenings we were never less than 4-persons as we walked around in the central areas without a worry. The second time two years later the situation was more unstable. I was there for a few days on my own and I only travelled about with Serge, our regular driver, who was very dependable although he only had about six words in English. His favourite expression to everything was "no problem" but his jovial approach to life was irresistible.

None of the Soviet block countries were members of the World Bank before the collapse of the USSR so there were no comparable data available prior to 1991. The per capita GNP for Kyrgyzstan that year was the equivalent of 1,160 Euro a sharp decline from earlier years, but in 1996 that figure had reduced to only 550 Euro which ranked among the lowest in Central Asia with the average rate of inflation 1985-1992 at 11.3%. Similarly social indicators such as mortality rates, child malnutrition and school attendance ratios had deteriorated. In the UNDP Human Development Index, the ranking of the Kyrgyz Republic fell from 26 of 173 countries in 1991 to 111 in 1996 and as a result of this rapid economic decline, much of the population faced severe hardship with average incomes down 65% in real terms from 1991 to 1995.

Under the Former Soviet Union, Kyrgyz had developed extensive health and education systems but the break-up of the FSU resulted in a steep economic recession and the transition to a market economy was accompanied by a sharp decrease in expenditure in these areas. The Government requested assistance to accelerate reform of critical social services in the two southern and isolated Provinces called Oblasts which had suffered the most. The agreed project aimed to improve the quality of life by promoting access and utilisation of basic social services for the vulnerable. The project proposed to support the rehabilitation of the health and education facilities including the upgrading of energy efficient design and materials in Osh and Jalal-Abad Oblasts where the Soviet system seemed incredibly wasteful and inefficient.

We stayed initially at the Dostok Hotel in Bishkek to work with the Government officials before leaving for the project areas in the south. The hotel was spacious and practical but with no colour, flowers, artwork or the concept of comfort we are used to in the West. With little money for utilities too, it was cold and inadequately lighted. There were security guards in the hall and a matron on each floor. The entrance hall was double height and each evening the mezzanine balcony had an abundance of "flowers of the night" or "les filles des joie" as the French would so beautifully put it. As economic hardship increases, so too the casualties and many of the ladies were married and often professional women trying to make a living to support their family while their husbands were unemployed. We were informed that of the 75 USD charge for their services, they got 25 USD and the balance was distributed between all levels of management and security that condone their presence.

We flew over the spectacular snow-capped Ferghana range in a Russian TU134 to Osh, the second city of c.250 000 population, in the south and worked for about 10 days in Osh and Jalal-Abad Oblasts. Osh dates from about the 5th century BC and was an important center on the Silk Road but is now a travellers' base for the Pamir Range. Here the people are a mixture of Kyrgyz and Uzbek and live around the very fertile Ferghana Valley. Stalin drew a line on the map, apparently without much ethnic consideration so that driving from Osh to Jalal-Abad, across the valley we

169

actually passed through about 10 km of Uzbekistan, retained by them because there was an hydro-electric dam there. Two years later in 2000 because of a worsening security situation, we were not allowed take this route through Uzbekistan and had to take an alternative barren mountain road about 80 km longer. This route was far less safe for us but our driver telephoned ahead regularly before proceeding. We stayed in a comfortable government rest house on hillside grounds securely fenced and 5 km outside Jalal-Abad overlooking the valley and fields of pistachio trees. It is a small resort town where until 1991, Russians came to take the waters at the Spa.

The staff had no resources but I negotiated a daily breakfast and advanced money to the cook each morning to get the necessary provisions for the subsequent meal. There were few bathrooms but a small communal pool could be used for washing and one of the staff arranged the rota each morning.

An US American consultancy firm with Bob Sanders as team leader was there to prepare the project for the Government and had established a project office in Jalal-Abad. The mission was timed to arrive for the completion of their work. It was obvious that the expatriates and Kyrgyz had worked very well together and each Friday evening after work they adjourned to a hostelry nearby. It was a basement bar accessed by descending steps with no natural light or ventilation. The walls, however, were covered with pictures of tropical islands, palm trees and golden beaches so the office had named the venue "Jamaica". Such social evenings were a wonderful way for getting to know the people who, since the work of that office was drawing to an end, they were apprehensive for their future. Every effort was being made to seek further employment for them but in that rapidly declining economy it was difficult to get anything even far below their qualifications.

They were a fun-loving people so as the second marriage of one women had just broken-up, it was suggested that since she had picked the first, the parents the second, she should now try procurement of the third by international competitive bidding to bank guidelines!!!

I visited in all about 25 health and education facilities including Raion hospitals, polyclinics, childrens' hospitals and outpatients clinics called Feldcher Accouch Points, which were the first level of primary health and maternity child health contact, as well as some fine schools from the Aravan and Kara-Su raions in Osh Oblast near the Fergana range north of Jalal-Abad.

Introducing a market economy including competitive bidding into a centralised system where as yet there was little or no private sector was a challenging exercise. The building activities from design, planning, services, construction trades, material quantities and costing all existed but in a command economy each is an independent element nominated by the State authority as required. The whole country was one large parastatal organisation. There were no competitions for the appointments so the costs are only known at the end. In our market economy the activities are grouped into Design Team for the pre-contract work and Building Contractors for the post-contract implementation which they win by competitive tendering based on common documents. Costs are then established in advance and can be controlled.

However, they had adjusted remarkably well so it was agreed that with a number of workshops, the working relationships between the different activities could be altered to suit the new Bank procurement requirements. I had discussions with the Oblast construction staff who were very competent but they had no resources, not even paper and pencils and the office had been run down to a skeleton staff. I met one engineer Nikolai Ulyankov, who had even come back from retirement to do some survey work without payment in order to help the project. The highest paid official was the senior architect at about 18 USD per month so obviously he, like the others, had to supplement his earnings with a second job in order to survive.

Our second visit originally planned for 1999 was delayed because of insurgency when hundreds of rebels invaded a remote area of southern Kyrgyzstan captured a number of villages and seized hostages. The 400 rebels were Uzbek Islamic militants from Tajikistan and Uzbekistan launched air-strikes against them. These were botched and some Kyrgyz civilians were killed and wounded, leading to Kyrgyz protests to Uzbekistan. Among the hostages kidnapped were 4 Japanese archaeologists who were working in the area. In their case, there was a suggestion that the Japanese government did pay the ransom demand before the captives were freed unharmed. If this payment was made it would make a good business of kidnapping, thereby increasing instability in the area and reducing the likelihood of the foreign investment essential to economic improvement. I would have to admit that if I were kidnapped I would like the Bank to pay a ransom to get me out, but I doubt they would. It took a number of months to resolve the hostage issue before we could return.

Between my first visit in 1998 and my second in 2000 it was sad to note the country had visibly further declined and the changes over the period had been traumatic. Cross-border travel in the area was more restricted, the currency has fallen by 180%, unemployment and crime had increased. I noted too that the invaluable Arabidin Abdulat, who accompanied me everywhere, used his mobile telephone constantly to ensure there were no new security problems ahead.

In these circumstances, the implementation of the project would be very difficult. A further problem also loomed large because loan money was not applicable to staff salaries. That part of the project implementation was the government contribution but if the staff were required to do the work without additional payment, the loss of the second job income and resulting hardship would almost inevitably lead to improper practices and corruption. Lurking in the background behind all these hardships and instability was an ever-present fear of a rise of Islamic fundamentalism.

Kyrgyzstan has all the qualities necessary for the development of a wonderful tourist industry with spectacular scenery, mountain trekking, mountaineering and sports for winter and summer. As yet, however, it lacks the necessary infrastructure and is only for the adventurous. The Kyrgyz are a friendly hospitable people and working in an official capacity in such countries, this time generally in a multi-discipline group of six, was a wonderful privilege. We got to know the local people at grassroots level in their everyday living while at the same time we were protected by our hosts from the many hassles and dangers experienced by the infrequent freelance tourist.

Perhaps the most dangerous situations we actually experienced however were the many dinners we attended. The Kyrgyz, Russians and it seems all the peoples of Central Asia partake of frequent 3 to 4 hour dinners at which everyone must propose at least one toast with often a long speech at the end of which one must finish the glass of vodka, which is then refilled for the next. Rising at 6.00am to go on a field-trip to visit health and education facilities in the rural areas, after such a dinner for 12 the evening before, I began to seriously question whether I was still suited to this way of life.

The mission ended successfully and on our last night in Jalal-Abad, we were taken to a local restaurant nearby which we had frequented often during our stay. That evening the cabaret ended with our Russian waitress singing us a special Russian farewell.

Tajikistan is approx the same latitude as Greece, Spain, Japan and Washington DC. It has frontiers with China, Afghanistan and a narrow strip of the latter separates it from India and Pakistan. 93% of the country is mountainous and almost half is over 3000 metres above sea level where most of the rivers of Central Asia have their origin.

Kalpak as Bus-stop, KyrgyzstanIsabel with her team, Tajikistan

TAJIKISTAN

After my first mission to Kyrgyzstan I returned to Central Asia in 1999, this time to Tajikistan for the preparation of another Social Sector Rehabilitation project. This was to be my last project of the century and I found the experience most unlike any other mission I have undertaken throughout Africa or Asia and one of the most enjoyable. We were a wonderful working group from Australia, New Zealand, Japan, Britain, Philippines, Nederlands and Ireland. The mission was led by Isabel Ortiz, a dynamic young lady from Spain.

Tajikistan was totally unprepared economically for the independence trust upon it. It was by far the weakest of the five new Republics and the most susceptible to the rise of Islamic forces in neighbouring Afghanistan to the south.

During the Soviet era, Moscow had been like the lid on a pressure cooker of clan-based tensions that had existed for a long time. With independence in 1991 the lid came off and civil war ensued claiming up to 50,000 lives and making refugees of half a million. The peace accord in 1997, between the government and opposition which ended the war, continued to face major breakdowns and outbursts of violence. The use of Tajikistan as a base by Iran and Russia for arms supplies to the anti-Taliban alliance in Afghanistan placed that fragile state in the front-line against the Taliban over the border and some months before our arrival, five United Nations observers were murdered just outside the capital Dushanbe. With Tajikistan also emerging

174

as a major export route for Afghan heroin, the role of the drug lords in de-stabilising the country increased.

Although there had been a precarious peace for the previous 12 months, fighting had not entirely ceased and most evenings we could hear gunfire some 3-5 kms distant and on one occasion, bazooka-like fire. However we did not feel immediately threatened at any time but our movements were very restricted and we were asked to confine ourselves, as much as possible, to a central triangular area. In this regard Patrick Devaney, Chief Administrator of the UN Military Observers in Tajikistan who was from Ireland was very helpful.

Needless to say the WB indicators showed Tajikistan very much behind the other Central Asian states with 80% of the people below the poverty line so the proposed project, very similar to that prepared the previous year in Kyrgyzstan, was even more greatly needed.

The country was just 'post-conflict' with an uneasy peace, so we did not fly in directly but through Tashkent. We were taken across the border from Uzbekistan in an United Nations convoy to the airport in the northern city of Khojan, from where we flew over the Tian-Shan Mountain ranges to the capital Dushanbe.

Dushanbe means Monday in Tajik because in ancient times the surrounding peoples came to the weekly market held on Mondays.The city, only about 80 years old, was now a modern urban centre with linear planning, tree-lined avenues and some fine buildings extensively landscaped. It was planned on the grand Russian manner with the principal Rudaki Avenue some 6 km. in length and possessing many fountains and larger-than-life sculptures. Tajikistan has a continental climate with minimal rainfall, hot summers up to 35 degrees in the lowlands and cold winters. May-June is the best time for moderate temperatures and a profusion of wild flowers, September-October for fruits.

Some of the more interesting buildings of Dushanbe included the National Library, the former House of Political Education, the Grand Restaurants and some terraces of town housing. One idea I liked was the Writers House with a museum of their works. Featured on an external front wall were the "stars of poetry", a sculptural composition of the busts of their greatest poets.

Originally we were to stay at the President's Dacha which was well fortified for security but for some reason we were never told, we were moved to the Oktyabrskaya / October Hotel on Rudaki Avenue. It too was planned in a grand manner with a suite for everyone but it was bare and lifeless although externally very well landscaped. We were given rooms on the first floor and security seemed tight. Helen McNaught our intrepid social sector specialist, was the only one allocated a ground floor room so we suggested she move up. She established that she was between two army generals so she decided to stay as she said she felt safe in the circumstances.
Because of the political instability too, the mission was unable to leave the city but the "tourist" architect did get out with the Deputy Minister for Health to visit some sites up to Hissar 30 km away where there are remains of an 18th century fortress and two Medressas. The Deputy Minister, an engineer by profession, initially seemed to me to be very sceptical of our activities but seemed quite relaxed about security although I noted that he did not go anywhere without two armed guards.
The existing health and education facilities were, in general, structurally sound with some evidence of roof frame deterioration but little serious wall cracking except for isolated positions. Essentially, the current poor condition of facilities arose from war damage and lack of building maintenance rather than any lack of construction capacity. Throughout the former Soviet Republics little attention seemed to be paid to energy efficiency in planning or the reduction of maintenance needs in the selection or use of materials so the project aimed to focus on these items also as part of the civil works.

In Dushanbe on one occasion after a meeting, I stopped off to visit an Historical and Art Museum, leaving the driver parked nearby in the shade.

When I returned some 40 minutes later, driver and car were gone so my interpreter, a daughter of one of the Ministers, insisted we make our way back quickly to the hotel by taxi. In the afternoon, the driver called to my hotel room to explain, he had been approached by 3 gunmen who demanded to be taken to Shartuz, on the Afghan border, 180 km to the south. Fortunately, driving through Dushanbe and passing the KGB Offices the driver recognised some friends. He pulled in quickly and called for assistance at which the gunmen panicked and fled.

The driver Batur was an example of the consequences of the changes occurring in the country. He was a university graduate in engineering and previously had a successful construction company. With the economic collapse, he had had to get the driving job to survive and so too had the other mission driver Baimatoff, who was a university trained nuclear engineer.

On another occasion some of the mission had a meeting at the President's Office and their interpreter arrived one hour late because of shooting in the street. That caused the mission some consternation although the Tajiks seemed to accept the delay as normal. In the meantime, although they had about 10 languages between both sides, they had none in common and were trying to conduct their business in words and signs until the interpreter eventually arrived.

Another day I got back to the hotel at lunch-time just as the United Tajik Opposition party leader was arriving to give a press conference. He had the support of the neighbouring Talaban in Afghanistan and I have never seen so many guns at such close quarters. I withdrew quickly to a Turkish restaurant across the street. There too were some men wearing the type of Pathan turban with which I wasfamiliar in Pakistan, not so far away across the mountains. The mission dined in that restaurant frequently and although run by Moslems, the waitress would send out for some beer for us provided we drank it discreetly.

The hotel did not have a restaurant as such but rather something like a boarding school refectory. One would think that it could not go far wrong for breakfast but it was never the same two days running. What one got was like a mystery tour with one item arriving at a time in any sequence. We tended to eat out in the evening but we only had 3-choices: the Turkish nearby, the UN rooftop canteen or the Indian restaurant attached to but not part of the Indian Embassy. The latter seemed to attract the relatively few expatriates and diplomats in the city. We would walk to these but even as a group we would watch the traffic, such as it was, and walk against the flow which seemed safer.

We saw armed police on Ruaki Avenue regularly, standing about every 100 meters to control traffic particularly if the President or a VIP was around. The control system was that if a vehicle was travelling too fast or infringing some rule, the policeman would fire one shot in the air. It was a very intimidating sound and had an immediate effect so I never heard a second shot being fired!

One of the highlights of my trip was meeting Batur's mother, Isaeva Sayera Junaidovna, the first Tajik woman architect. She had been specially selected on the basis of her school results for architectural training in St. Petersburg, then Leningrad, in the early 1950s. She returned to Dushanbe in 1960 and worked on housing, then specialised in the urban planning of the suburbs of the capital and the provincial cities and towns of Tajikistan. She and her husband, a retired Senior Engineer in the Ministry, were delightful and I was honoured to be invited to a family birthday celebration meal complete with vodka toasts in their house with Batur's wife and children. Living in a good quality 2-bedroom apartment, by Western standards, she was now retired also and her special joy was looking after her six grand-children. At the end of the meal Isaeva presented me with a book on the Architecture of the Soviet Tadjikistan.

The mission never spoke or seemed conscious of a threatening danger although looking back later we must have subconsciously been on our guard all the time. The preparation of a project usually took two or even three visits but this project was relatively small and because of the fragile nature of the society, we were to carry out the full preparation in one mission. Isabel had a wonderful way of binding us together as a unit. She bought a bust of Lenin which she displayed on the table at each of our meetings and would start each time with "Lenin thinks we should -------"and we worked enthusiastically in an atmosphere of simple light relief. This concentration on work in a lighter atmosphere seemed to permeate all expatriates in Dushanbe and probably relieved the tension. The irrepressible Greek National Basil Comnas was always in good form. He headed up a multi-sector program for the UN and other donors supporting the restoration of basic conditions for the sustainable human development in order to support the fragile peace.

At the end of the mission, we returned to Khojan by the small Yak 40. The airplane rose in a number of circles to gain sufficient height to cross over the surrounding mountains. The UN convoy then took us across the frontier into Uzbekistan. It was with some relief that we set off, across the plains and collective farms to Tashkent in Uzbekistan as the mountains of Tajikistan faded behind us.

Tashkent was the largest city, the hub of Central Asia and in spite of its ups and downs over the centuries has remained the cross-roads of international trade and a centre of art and culture with numerous theatres, art galleries, museums and academies. It was among the largest of the Soviet cities, with a metro and some marvellous modern architecture in which architects tried to take account of national traditions in their facades and decoration. I liked the city, Chorsu market was an "Aladdin's cave" and dining out on Sailqakh Street called "Broadway" locally, in the centre of the city was a wonderful spot to watch the Central Asian world go by.

THE GREAT SILK ROUTE

The trade route known as "the Silk Road" once took this Central Asian route from China in the east to the shores of the Mediterranean in the west, transporting goods, people, ideas and religions from one end of the Eurasian land-mass to the other. The well-worn trails were used for centuries by caravan traders such as Marco Polo and conquerors like Ghengis Khan and Tamerlane, but have since remained off the beaten path for travellers and tourists for centuries. From western China, the trail divided and took differing routes through the valleys of the Pamir and Tian-Shan ranges, through present day Kyrgyzstan and Tajikistan, but these joined again in southern Uzbekistan.

From Tashkent I set off with a translator Olga Khaberkhanova to visit the famous city of Samarkand some 300 kms distant. A year later Olga visited our friends Derry and Anne O'Connor in Galway and we were able to reciprocate her hospitality by taking her for a cruise on the River Shannon. The driver and guide Rustam Umarov knew Samarkand well, a city of 400,000 population and one of the oldest cities in the world with 25 centuries of history - a city of legends where European and Asiatic architecture combine. Samarkand has been fixed in western popular imagination by poets and playwrights and imortalised by James Flecher's 1913 poem which concludes; "-------- for lust of knowing what should not be known, we take the golden road to Samarkand". It has withstood the armies of Alexander the Great, Arab Caliphate, Ghengis Khan and his descendent, Timur the Great called Tamerlane who gathered his army there, planning to make Samarkand the capital of the world. To stress its importance he named the towns around it: Baghdad, Shiraz, Misr (Cairo) and these names have largely held to this day. Majestic and beautiful, Samarkand was known as the "the Rome of the East", the pearl of the Eastern Moslem world and the major city on the Great Silk Road.

Our first stop was at the 15th century Gur Emir Mausoleum, a one cupola building with a crypt which contains the dark green nephrite tombstone over the grave of Tamerlane, together with the marble tombstones of his sons, grandsons and family. The Octahedral building carries a highly decorated cylindrical drum crowned by a hugh azure-fluted dome against a background of terracotta brickwork. The majesty of architectural forms, lines and colourful mosaics distinguishes it as one of the unique monuments of mediaeval architecture. The Shakhi-Zinda complex of memorial and religious buildings to the north-east is perhaps the most important necropolis of Central Asia, in which one finds many varieties and types of ceramic designs, glazed terracotta, painted majolica, carved mosaic and murals.

Registan Square – Samarkand, Uzbekistan

However, Registan Square has formed the heart of the ancient Samarkand and centre of the most majestic sight of Central Asia. It is a unique example of town building art and a remarkable pattern of the architectural planning of the main town square, surrounded by 3 monumental Medressa; the 15th century Ulugbek to the West, Sher Dor to the east and the beautiful Tilla-Kari in the centre, the latter from the 17th century. The Medressa is the highest religious institution combined with an Academy and the Registan ensemble leaves an unforgettable impression. "Tilla-Kari" means "gold covered" and the interior of the dome is particularly beautiful. The Tilla-Kari Medressa was the University as well as the Cathedral Mosque of the Registan, the focal point of Samarkand which, in turn, was the cultural centre of the ancient state.

There were many other buildings of note; Bibi-Khanym mosque, Ulughbek observatory, etc and having received independence in 1991, Uzbekistan embarked on extensive restoration works to all their cultural shrines, buildings and artwork. At the same time, through the efforts of the World Tourism and Trade Organisations, UNESCO and the Silk Road Countries from China to Greece joined together to promote tourism along this historic route. The collapse of communism has then reopened to the world a major culture which we were beginning to forget ever existed.

I have visited four of the republics of the FSU and having worked in the social sectors of health and education in Kyrgyzstan and Tajikistan over the three years 1998 to 2000, I have been privileged to experience and learn something of their way of life throughout the years that the whole vast area was closed to the outside world. Essentially, Central Asia was an area of transit for the many passing ethno-linguistic groups; Slavic, Persian, Mongolian, Turkic, Indo-European and other categories. The two principal powers of the area although closely akin represented the two very differing lifestyles. One was nomadic and pastoral in which the Kazak herders flourished and as a united group or horde, established what was probably to be the last nomadic empire. The second was sedentary agriculture, which the Uzbeks developed in the fertile valleys they settled. This settled life, led to the establishment of such great cities as Bhukara, Khiva and especially Samarkand. Following a period of decline in the 19th century it was finally subdued by the Red Army Commander Frunze, following the Bolshevik Revolution.

The forced collectivisation policy of the 1920s put an end to the wandering lifestyle of the Kazak and literally, millions died. The depopulated steppe, were seen as and became good real-estate for Russian expansion. The Kyrgyz, who are ethnically very close to the Kazaks, were driven south to the Tien-Shan Mountains and in time were also subdued by the Red Army. The Tajiks, the oldest settled inhabitants who are ethnically Persian, were the least prepared for nationhood or subsequent independence and descended immediately into civil war.

In spite of disastrous agricultural policies, environmental destruction and appalling repression of the people, the Soviet Era was seen as a beneficial time. The area was improved profoundly, with health care, education and vast new infrastructure which reached all social levels, so their overall standards of living were raised considerably. Artistic expression was encouraged too and through the arts, the republics were allowed to develop their own distinctive national traditions and identities, all strictly within the perimeters of the communist ideology.

The collapse in 1991 was then traumatic and as an example the experiences of one Russian colleague, Nina illustrates the contrasts: born and grown-up in Frunze now Bishkek she was selected and sent to be educated at the University of Tomsk. After a number of successful years experience in engineering, she returned to Frunze. Bright, educated and ambitious she quickly rose to a well-paid managerial position in a state company. A good life with nice apartment and car seemed assured but with the collapse of communism everything changed.

Today she needs at least 2-jobs to survive; secretarial and cleaning employment, often working 12-hours per day and with only 2-days off per month, her standard of living is a fraction of that of the 1980s. Although earning perhaps up to150 USD per month she is doing very well by Kyrgyz standards.

City names too are changing from Russian to Kyrgyz, Kazak, Uzbek and Tajik and if Central Asia follows the normal pattern of evolving states and there is no evidence to suggest otherwise, increasing unemployment with consequent hardship could lead to local resentment of their better-off Russian fellow citizens. The resulting insecurity and fear that one day they may have to flee becomes a compelling motive to work and earn the maximum as quickly as possible. Their situation is I think very similar to that of the European settlers in Africa. After all that, our earlier trip to Russia itself took on a whole new significance.

Following the excitement in the West at the fall of Communism in Russia in August 1991, we went to Moscow in the summer of 1992. We hoped to see the countryside so we chose a cruise sailing from Moscow to St. Petersburg as it had the advantage that once we got on board into our cabin we did not have to live out of a suitcase for the two weeks. The route from Moscow took us by the Moscow Canal to the Volga River visiting Uglich and Yaroslavl, north through the Rybinsk reservoir to the Baltic Canal to Lake Onega, Lake Ladoga and Svir River to St. Petersburg.

We started from Moscow and at the southern end of the Red Square stands the Cathedral of Saint Basil. This richly and gaily decorated Church, with it's wonderfully distinctive onion domes, is probably the most powerful symbol of Russia. Architecturally, I think the quieter beauty of the buildings around Cathedral Square in the Kremlin is more appealing. The artwork in the Kremlin Palace is very rich in colour and detail but of all the Cathedrals in the Kremlin, the Cathedral of the Dormition is the outstanding building of the entire complex. The austere grandeur of the embellishments outside is a beautiful envelope for the richly decorated interior.

The old and distinctive Russian architecture of the "Golden Ring" particularly in Suzdal which has some lovely wooden churches was a wonderful experience. In Zagorsk, too the holiest of cities soon to be renamed Seriyev Posad and the place of Orthodox pilgrimage where even the tsars had to approach on foot was especially noteworthy.

Costs seemed reasonable on the boat for everything except for coffee and beer so I naively thought I would buy some coffee and a six-pack. In Uglich I tried to find a shop but walked into living rooms and kitchens before I eventually found one. There was no advertising so for a stranger there was no way of knowing. The shop was a sad sight as most shelves were empty. The proprietor seemed overwhelmed at my presence but without a common language all we could do was smile and nod to one another.

The multiple-domed church on Kizhi Island in Lake Onega, was built entirely of timber without the use of nails but we were unable to go inside as it was undergoing maintenance works. It is included on the World Heritage list by the United Nations Educational, Scientific and Cultural

Organisation as are the Hermitage, Churches and Historic Centre of St. Petersburg.

At the end of the cruise some passengers were commenting that they had never been in so many churches in their life, which was really saying a lot about Russia culturally. Much of the visual art, architecture and iconography to which people can relate, is rooted in their Christian Orthodox tradition. We were probably a bit too soon after the political collapse with our visit because many buildings including the Tretiakov Gallery were to undergo upgrading before they could be made available to visitors. When a place has to be renovated in Russia, it seems they simply close it so that nothing in it is available to the public maybe for a period of up to five years. They do not seem to make temporary arrangements to facilitate the convenience of the public.

INTERNATIONAL AID

The world of Development Aid was one I stumbled into by chance although in retrospect it followed naturally from our years in Africa.

Architects provide their services either as implementing consultants providing the normal architectural service for the design and supervision of buildings from conception to realisation or alternatively as a project consultant for the financier using experience previously gained in implementation.

I had worked as the former for over 20 years and I first set out to work overseas in the same way. In 1975 I was recommended for projects in Africa under the European ACP Africa, Caribbean & Pacific Lome Convention. I travelled to Africa to follow-up this work but found it costly, unrewarding and frustrating, so I turned to consultancy for the financiers. In October 1977, Dympna and I went to the US for a holiday and spent a few days in Washington DC. I was familiar with the Bank and the possibilities that could arise for consultants with my experience of the Developing World. Accordingly with the help of Ireland's Coras Trachtala

Executive Director Donal Scully thatvisit led to a relationship which was to take me throughout Africa and Asia over the following 24 years.

Bank staff seemed to have similar background experience as myself, having worked and lived in the Third World either with colonial, post-colonial administrations, bilateral aid agencies, non-government organizations or the peace-corps and this common currency was a great help.

The World Bank is a Development Institution owned by the Member countries. The name WB refers to two legally and financially distinct entities: International Bank for Reconstruction and Development IBRD and International Development Association IDA. The IBRD began in 1946 and finances its lending operations by borrowing in world capital markets. The interest rates and repayment periods of IBRD loans are generally more favourable than members can obtain from commercial banks. The IDA began in 1960 and assists the poorest developing members out of resources provided by the wealthier countries. IDA credits are interest free and have longer repayment periods.

Concession credits carry only service charges of 0.75 to 1 % per year repayable over 35 to 40 years including a grace period of 10 years. DMCs only borrow for the foreign exchange portion of the project.

The International Finance Corporation IFC began in 1956 and is an affiliate of the WB. It seeks to promote growth in developing members' private sectors by mobilising foreign and domestic capital to invest alongside its own funds in commercial enterprises.

The WB Group includes the Multilateral Investment Guarantee Agency MIGA and the International Centre for Settlement of Investment Disputes ICSID. The Group was established with the International Monetary Fund IMF (the Fund) in 1945 to help raise standards in developing countries.

Borrowing countries have full responsibility for the design, preparation and implementation of individual projects but the WB is deeply involved in each of these stages.

Once a project has been identified as having a high priority for the economic development of the country, it undergoes intensive preparation by the borrower and the bank to ensure that it is soundly designed, properly organised and up to standards of economy and efficiency. The project stages are illustrated in the diagram above.

My initial missions were simple project supervision but in time my Terms of Reference expanded to encompass preparation, appraisal and supervision in the social sectors of health and education.

Even though a preparation mission could be intense they usually proved the more satisfying because there was a real sense of achievement in collaborating with the Borrower to design a brand new project. It never ceased to amaze me how a group of six or eight people of different disciplines and nationalities, who had never met before, could come together and work closely for weeks and successfully create a new project.

The Multi-National lending agencies grant loans or credits to their own members in accordance with criteria set by their governing body, appointed from their members. The loans are usually made for carefully identified projects, prepared, appraised and agreed. Implementation is supervised and on completion the overall project is evaluated. At appraisal stage, a comprehensive review of all aspects of the project, including its possible environmental impact, is undertaken. The project then goes to the Government and Bank Board for approvals on receipt of which the loan effective date is set and the Staff Appraisal Report SAR becomes the guiding document for project implementation. There may be a formal project launch, sometimes with a workshop to assist project success.

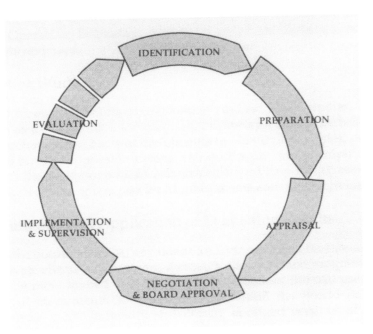

World Bank Project Cycle

I thought the thoroughness with which these projects were prepared was very impressive. A macro-economic review would be undertaken to establish the breakdown of National expenditure and a micro-economic evaluation of all the health and education costs to ensure that the country could sustain the project. For example, in a Primary Health or Maternity Child Health Project, all the services to be delivered would first be listed - medical, surgical, maternity, ante/post natal, nutritional, immunisation, etc., followed by tables of the necessary staff, equipment and essential drugs. The accounting, management and training resources at every level would be included.

The architect would prepare accommodation models for each service and would arrange the necessary surveys and mapping to establish where facilities exist.Their accommodation and condition would be established in order to see the spread and quality of the existing health services.

In the meantime field-trips would establish sample needs of indicative works and costs as a guide. This would be followed by policy decisions on the density of facilities to be addressed based on say population criteria from which the volume of necessary rehabilitation was established. The project document is then drafted to show the individual components, the strategy and program for realisation and the overall project cost estimates. It would be updated during subsequent missions as the detailed knowledge of each of the resources was established. Projects might include institutional development, an awareness component, education workshops and communication programs. Provisions are made for policy research and cost recovery to ensure sustainability and maintenance of facilities and equipment. Projects were designed with clear objectives so that their effectiveness can be evaluated in advance and measured during progress. On completion, project performance would be evaluated and lessonslearned.

Ideally I think the same personnel should stay with a project during implementation but, while I have been lucky to be asked to stay with a few projects through supervision, that is not the norm probably because of the time taken for projects to run their full course.

I always felt that supervision was not given the same priority as preparation. There was often an unavoidable delay between preparation and implementation and I fear that some project momentum was lost in that time. It could be further aggravated by changes of personnel at both donor and borrower levels. The more successful projects, I thought, were those where much the same personnel continued from project inception through at least the early years of implementation. The initial project-launch, together with the first couple of years of implementation are critical periods during which time teething problems and modalities can be ironed out. Close attention to the successful completion of the early components could set the standard for the entire project.

Lack of maintenance and bad governance is a major problem.

I found it very sad to return in 1992 to see Nigeria borrowing for a health referral project, the aim of which, I thought,was essentially to bring the health services back to the level that they had been in the 1960s. That prompts the question as to what is the long term benefit of the WB projects. RegretfullyI think, if a majority of projects achieved a minority of targets over some of their components, the work was well worthwhile.

Development Aid is very different to the humanitarian response to human catastrophes known as Emergency Aid. The latter became a feature of the 20th century in contrast to the laissez faire philosophy of the 19th century which was applied for example by the British Government during the Irish famine.

Other International lending agencies include the Regional Development Banks in Asia ADB, Africa AfDB and the Inter-America Bank They confine their activities to their Developing Member Countries (DMCs) in their own areas. The European Union, Organisation of Petroleum Exporting Countries and most developed countries run programs of bilateral aid and grants for development and emergency purposes.

The loans are given to Governments in instalments, the number and size of which depends on the size and type of project. The first tranche is paid to the Treasury/Ministry of Finance of the Borrower who in turn passes it to the implementing ministry; health, education, etc. They spend it on the project and when used, a Bank supervision mission visits to ensure procurement and implementation compliance with the Loan Agreement. When the Bank is satisfied, the second tranche is issued and so on until project completion.

The Bank also provides a wide range of technical assistance services for which they charge.

The volume of this aid world-wide is staggering, for example the World Bank approved some 15 billion USDs for new projects in 1999 with 25% contribution from the USA and Japan followed by Germany, France and Britain. The same year the ADB approved 5 billion USDs with 30% from the

USA and Japan. Other donors include China, India, Korea, Indonesia, Australia and Canada.

With the collapse of communism and growth of communications making the world a smaller place, the demands for aid grew enormously. It would seem too that the needs of the Developing World might now be more easily addressed at Regional level so that I would expect the Asian, African and Inter-American Banks to assume a greater role in their respective regions in future. The World Bank and International Monetary Fund may then play a more specialist role in World Development, perhaps in greater partnership with the private sector. However, in all my travels I never found a crystal ball.

The WB tends to take stock of its performance every 10 years and carry out a major overhaul of its resources which is very unsettling for the staff. Of course such fundamental soul-searching prevents the institution from getting into a too "comfortable groove".

Because the Developed World's resources are limited compared to the demands, aid must be prioritised and it is noted that the multinational lending agencies have since the year 2000 set Poverty Alleviation as the central criteria for project selection. However the methods seem to vary with the changes of Administration in the United States. Social issues seem to have a lower priority during a Republican Presidency and greater budget reductions are applied in the health and education areas. The use of the private sector by the DMCs and paid for by the Agencies, for the preparation of projects has increased. Contracts are awarded on a competitive basis and it was in this way that I went to Lesotho as part of the successful bidding of the Boston University Centre for the International Health team

Although my work in this field was part-time, my main work being the running of a private architect's practice at home in Ireland, it played a very important part in our lives. I found the people involved very caring. They

191

genuinely sought to assist the Developing Countries in every way and we did feel we were giving valuable assistance.

I obviously had a very strong desire to see the world so it was wonderful to be actually paid to do it in this privileged and beneficial way for others as well as myself. I never really had any worry travelling abroad even on my own or in strange environments as I always tried to relate to some familiar cultural activity.

The obvious one was the building industry but I have also sought out a golf club or the Church as they could provide familiar moments of light relief. One Sunday in Capetown, Andy Beggs and I went to a church and at the end of the service the parish priest invited the congregation to the community hall for refreshments. Although strangers we went along. The occasion was to bid farewell to a curate who was being transferred to another parish. The curate made a good witty parting speech at the end of which Andy leaned over to say he would miss the priest and was sorry he was leaving.

Unlike the rest of sub-Saharan Africa, the RSA is part of the Developed World and with the ending of the apartheid in 1994 a new complex social system is emerging as the 20th century ends. I am very thankful for the opportunities I've had in this field and for the wonderful variety of colleagues with whom I've worked on such worthwhile projects over 40 missions in 18 developing countries.

CONCLUSION

My journey to the Developing World began on the m.v. Aureol and her life makes an interesting analogy with the latter half of the century. Named after Mount Aureol in Sierra Leone, the keel was laid in Glasgow in 1949 and her maiden voyage was from Britain to West Africa in 1951. She served as a regular liner on that route, completing over 200 round voyages, until 1974. She was then sold, renamed Marianna VI and put into service as an accommodation ship at Jeddah and later as an hotel ship at

Rabegh where she remained until 1989. Laid up in Piraeus until 2001, it was finally broken up in India.

The old Chinese wish *"that you may live in interesting times"* could be applied to the 20th century. The first half saw 2 appalling world wars separated by a world economic collapse. The second half brought an end to colonialism and the growth of independent nation members of the United Nations Organisation from 60 in 1950 to over 180 by the year 2000. From the Russian Revolution of 1917 Communism expanded to envelope half the world until the collapse of the USSR in 1991 with the emergence of new nations in Central Asia.

The 20th century saw art and architecture move from the classical revival styles to a series of more radical forms. From Art Nouveau and the Bauhaus, modern styles continued to be influenced by great individual architects such as Frank Lloyd Wright, Le Corbusier and Mies van der Rohe. Opinions, of course, will vary but my personal choice of building hallmarks of the century must include the Sydney Opera House by the Danish architect Jorn Utzon who won an international design competition for it and the Nossa Senhora Aparecida Cathedral of Brasilia in which concrete and glass are beautifully woven by the architect Oscar Niemeyer.
All forms of technology advanced enormously in the final decades with instant communications, personal computers, the internet, inter-continental travel and higher living standards becoming attainable worldwide and extendable in time from the Developed World.

In Europe the century was spent coming to terms with itself and Germany which had been unified in 1871 by Bismarck. It was not until 1952 that the peaceful integration of the continent began with the signing of the Treaty forming the Coal and Steel Community by the 6 founding members France, Germany, Italy and Benelux. Ireland joined the European Community in 1973. By the end of the century the European Union had expanded to 15 countries of which 12, including Ireland had formed the Single Euro Currency Zone and negotiations for entry early in the 21st century had commenced with 12 further Central and Eastern European countries.

Cathedral of Brasilia, Brazil 1959

Ireland entered the 20th century with an unwelcome British dimension which was partly removed in 1920. The educational focus then became the promotion of Irish culture and the de-anglicising of the country. The architecture and development of the towns as the normal visual and social expression of the culture of the people had been distorted and took three generations to reverse. It was not until the final decades of the century that Ireland, although still handicapped by the partition of the country, could finally take its place culturally and economically in Europe as the 30 years war in the north-east moved into a peace process.

As we enter the 21st century the country is in transition so that the realisation of a unified Ireland of 6 million people in the unified Europe, from the Atlantic to the Urals as envisaged by Charles de Gaulle, seems attainable. Everything looked reasonably optimistic for the future as our grandchildren arrived to the 21st century but then in September 2001 members of the Islamic al-Qa'ida organisation high-jacked some scheduled airplanes and in suicide operations crashed into and destroyed the World Trade Towers in New York and part of the Pentagon in Washington DC killing all passengers and nearly three thousand innocent people in the buildings.

In 2002 too when I was working with the Boston University team in Lesotho, I became painfully aware of the terrible consequences of HIV/AIDS in Southern Africa. In Lesotho the 1996 census projection for the following 30 years showed a population increase from 1.9 million to 3.6 million in 2026. However, when allowance was made for the expected mortality arising from AIDS, this latter figure reduced to 2.4 million. In every country of Southern Africa there is a severe AIDS epidemic and life expectancy was falling dramatically from near 60 years to 40, sometimes even lower. At a Saint Patrick's Day reception at the Irish Consulate in Maseru I met a missionary priest who said that they had so many funerals each week that he had to train one of his lay assistants to take some of them as he could not cope alone.

These occurrences together with the reactions to them internationally make the immediate future more uncertain and I am reminded of another old Chinese proverb;

"unless we change direction, we are likely to end up where we are headed "

I wonder if this period of history; the collapse of communism, the triumph of global capitalism and the September 11-2001 attacks will turn out to be one of those periods of history that our grandchildren will look back on and say that they changed the direction of the world.

As we enter the 21st century it is interesting to note that if we could shrink the earth's population to a village of 100 people, with the existing human ratios remaining, it would be made up of the following types;

57 Asians

21 Europeans

14 Americans - North & South

  8 Africans

70 would be non-white and non-Christian

11 would be homosexual

  6 would possess 59% of the world's wealth, all 6 from USA

80 would live in substandard housing

70 would be unable to read

50 would suffer from malnutrition

  1 would have a college education

However, given the momentum created by the rate of positive development in the latter half of the 20th century, the prospects for the 21st century must be very encouraging. Perhaps one of our grandchildren, in the autumn of their lives, will take up their pencil and continue from this journal to write the story of their century.

NFCB

Printed in Poland
by Amazon Fulfillment
Poland Sp. z o.o., Wrocław

56475243R00116